Tl

The Horizon Press

The Old House, Hereford

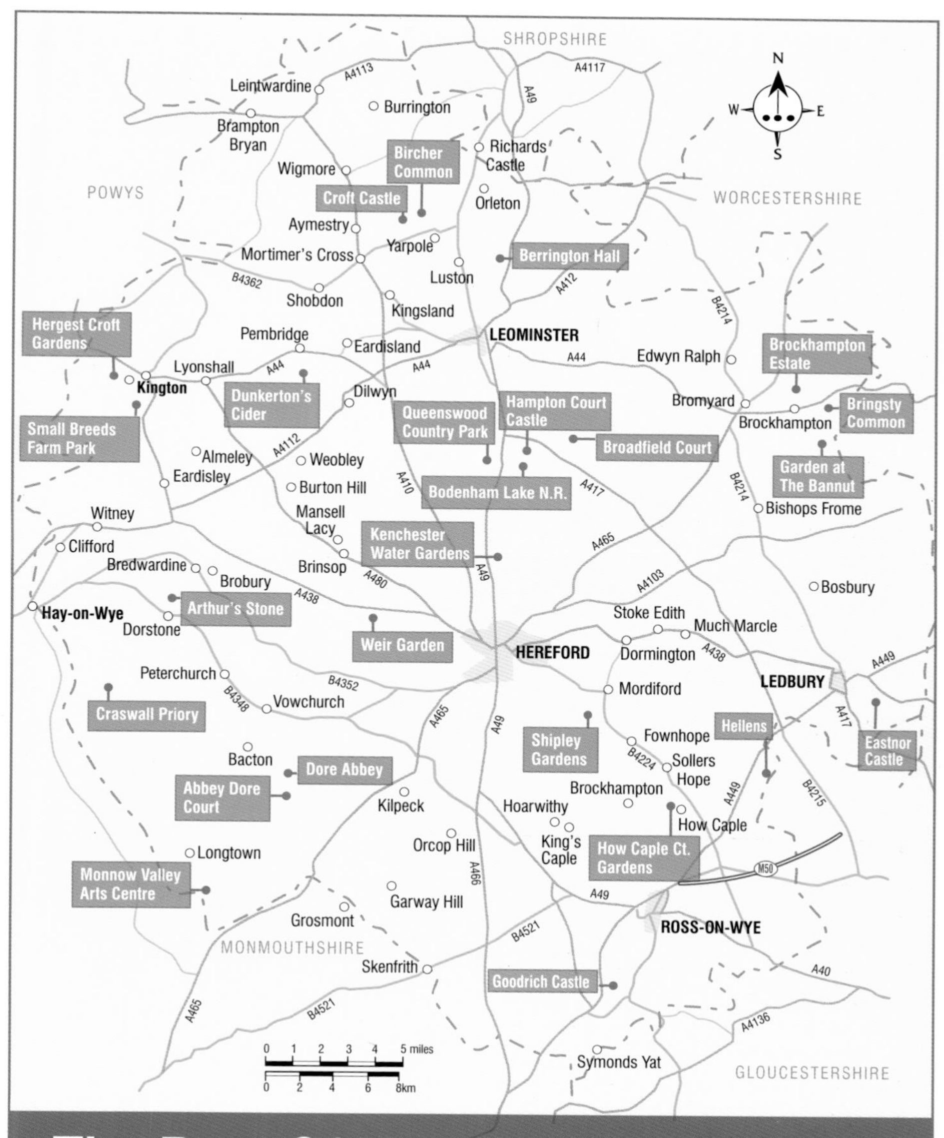

The Best Of Herefordshire

The Bannut temporarily closed
How Caple Garden permanently closed
2014

Contents

Welcome to

The Best of Herefordshire

Herefordshire is one of England's most rural counties, with a population less than that of many cities and some large towns. To traverse the county is a matter of covering a mere forty miles or so but set within its borders is the varied landscape of hills, river valleys, market towns, farmland and historic buildings which many consider to be the England of popular imagination.

At its heart, both administratively and historically, is the cathedral city of Hereford, with the only other urban centres being the market towns of Kington, Leominster, Bromyard, Ledbury and Ross-on-Wye. There are also five major rivers, the Teme, Lugg and Arrow in the northern half of the county, the Frome in the east, and the major waterway of the Wye in the west and south. Although

Opposite page: Grange Court, Leominster
Left: Station sign, Ledbury

Top Tips

Brockhampton Estate and Lower Brockhampton
Country estate and moated manor house with walks and trails

Croft Castle
17th century castellated mansion and gardens, with parkland and walks

Dore Abbey
Former Cistercian monastery founded by French monks in the 12th century

Eastnor Castle
Fairytale castle, deer park, arboretum and lake with maze and adventure playground

Goodrich Castle
11th century castle set on wooded hill above the picturesque River Wye

Hampton Court Castle and Gardens
Historic house, gardens and parkland

Hellens
Manor House and gardens containing a wealth of period furnishings, paintings and decorations

Hereford Cathedral
Historic building with Mappa Mundi exhibition and Chained Library

Goodrich Castle

Hergest Croft Gardens
Family managed garden with 5,000 rare trees and shrubs with views to the Black Mountains

Shortwood Family Farm
Organic working dairy farm with farm tours, hands-on activities and friendly animals

Waterworks Museum
History of drinking water explained through working engines, displays and films

Wye Valley Walk
Herefordshire section of this waymarked route passes through some of the county's best countryside

Hereford Cattle

However you travel through Herefordshire, whether by bike, train, car, or on foot, you are sure to see the famous white faces and red coats of Hereford cattle. Tradition has it that the Hereford Breed traces its origins from the Red Cattle, which used to have free rein along the lands either side of the Welsh and English border and it was as long ago as the seventeenth and eighteenth centuries that mention began to be made of the breed which came to be known as the Hereford.

However, formal records only began in the 1800s with the publication of Herd Books. The first Herd Book of Hereford Cattle was published in 1846 and contained the records of over 500 bulls and their breeders. A Hereford Herd Book Society was formed in the 1870s and it is still in existence today, known as The Hereford Cattle Society. In 1886 the Herd Book was closed to any animal whose ancestry had not previously been recorded, with the purpose of maintaining the purity of the breed. Since the ancestry of Hereford cattle was first recorded, the breed has been exported to over twenty countries around the world, including the United States and Australia.

The reasons for the breed's success has been attributed to many aspects, such as its foraging ability, its docile behaviour, its ease of calving and fertility. Not least though is its traceability, as throughout its history the Hereford has maintained the distinctive white face and red coat and, in addition, all cross-bred Hereford cattle maintain a white face, a distinct advantage for tracing identity. Lastly, the Hereford is praised for producing excellent 'marbled' beef, which has a distinctive flavour and enables the meat to command a premium price.

these rivers now lend charm to the rural nature of the landscape, they were once integral to the commerce and traffic of those living in the county.

The road system has contributed to this feeling of rural seclusion and includes only one short stretch of motorway, the M50, known originally as the Ross Spur, which links the county to the busy motorways of the Midlands and the A40 into Wales. Dividing the county from north to south is the main trunk road of the A49, while only two major roads cross the county east to west, the A44 through Leominster and the A438 through Hereford. Herefordshire contains no significant industrial conurbations and, in a sense, could be said to have avoided many of the horrors of the Industrial Revolution of the eighteenth and nineteenth centuries and the associated post-industrial problems of decline and regeneration that have plagued and challenged the neighbouring areas of the Midlands and South Wales.

However, this should not eclipse the historical significance of Herefordshire as a thoroughfare and trading centre since medieval times. The county is criss-crossed by the remnants of Roman roads, Celtic trackways, old drovers' routes, canals, tramroads and railways, all of which in their time saw the passage of people, merchandise, and livestock destined for the markets and major cities of England and beyond. There is a plethora of villages with a substantial church which can date its foundation to Norman or even Saxon times and many of the pubs and inns have been serving travellers and locals for over half a millennium. In addition, there is substantial archaeological evidence of significant occupation stretching back to Neolithic times.

For centuries the Marcher Lords fought themselves and the Welsh for control of the rich agricultural land that dominates the area to the east of the border of Wales and England, and travelling about the county there is the impression that farming is still very much at the heart of the countryside, despite the undoubted pressures and difficulties facing farmers in the twenty-first century. Over hundreds of years of breeding, the white faces and red coats of Herefordshire cattle have become well known for their docile behaviour, fertility, and hardiness. Leominster was the home of the Ryeland sheep, sought after for the softness of its wool, and since medieval times, until wool was superseded by cotton, it accounted for a significant part of that town's wealth. The county's orchards and hop fields have long been cultivated for the production of cider, perry and beer, and, though the twentieth century saw a significant decline in the number of acres planted with these crops, there is now something of a revival among small and large-scale producers alike, with Bulmers of Hereford claiming to be largest cider-maker in the world.

About this Guide

This guide is divided into four areas – Hereford and the South; Ledbury, Bromyard and the East; Leominster and the North; Kington and the West. The decision of where to draw the boundaries between the areas is somewhat artificial, but has largely been dictated by the spread of the county's towns and its topography. Selecting entries for inclusion has largely been made on the basis of what Herefordshire best has to offer the visitor. Certain places have been mentioned because they are particular to this part of the world or because not to have mentioned them would have been neglectful, but many have been included simply because they caught the author's eye and imagination. However, this is in no way a claim for a comprehensive or definitive guide, but if it gives a first insight into what there is to see I hope it will have served its purpose. For those wanting more detailed explanations and histories there is a wealth of books and pamphlets about different aspects of the county to be found in local libraries and bookshops.

Above: High Street, Ledbury

Left: Bromyard Folk Festival

Walking in Herefordshire

The county has over 2,000 miles of public footpaths and other rights of way as well as a number of fully waymarked linear and circular trails. The terrain is varied, with upland areas, river valleys, old commons and heaths, woodland, town and country parks and farmland dotted with villages, pubs, tearooms, and churches. The only thing the county lacks for variety is a coastline. Listed below are some of the main areas for walking, though pleasant short walks and strolls can be found from almost any village or town.

Walking Areas

Hereford and the South: the River Wye dominates the landscape in the south of the county and forms the core of the Wye Valley Area of Outstanding Natural Beauty. Immediately below Hereford the Wye meanders through the floodplains and makes for excellent walking in the summer months. However, from Goodrich onwards the river enters a limestone gorge, more reminiscent of one of the great continental rivers of Europe, and passes through the dramatic cliffs of Coldwell Rocks, Yat Rock, and the Seven Sisters. Meanwhile to the southwest of Hereford is the ancient area of Archenfield, with its rolling hills of scattered woods and fields among small hidden valleys.

The East: to the east of Hereford are the steep slopes of the Woolhope Dome, rising to over 250m above the Wye Valley and a haven for wildlife. It is an area of national importance for its botanical and geological aspects. Beyond Ledbury, are the Malvern Hills, another Area of Outstanding Natural Beauty, which extend in an undulating spine along the county border. To the north, near Bromyard, are the smaller, though no less enticing, former commons of Bringsty and the Bromyard Downs, which give gentle walking at any time of the year.

The North: Queenswood Country Park, between Hereford and Leominster, has a network of woodland trails, some of which are suitable for wheelchairs and buggies. In the northwest of the county are the upland commons and steep-sided valleys of the Mortimer Forest and the old Radnor Hills, extending north and west into Shropshire and Wales.

The West: Bradnor Hill and Hergest Ridge near Kington draw many walkers and the town has in recent years promoted itself as a centre for walking. Further south, at Hay, the River Wye passes from hill country into farmland of fields and old orchards on its way to Hereford. However, the main walking area in this part of the county is the Black Mountains, whose northern ridges form the southwestern border. The northern tops of Hay Bluff and Black Hill are within the reach of most walkers, though the higher parts to the south can take on the character of serious hills at certain times of the year, requiring proper route-finding skills.

Longer Trails

The Herefordshire Trail: 150 mile circular route through the county, linking the market towns of Leominster, Bromyard, Ledbury, Ross and Kington.

Wye Valley Walk: more than a third of this waymarked trail passes through the county from Hay in the west, via Hereford, to Symonds Yat in the south.

Offa's Dyke Path: a significant section of this national trail passes along or near the county border, from the Black Mountains in the south through Hay-on-Wye to Kington and beyond.

The Mortimer Trail: a 30 mile route linking the towns of Ludlow and Kington, passing through an area dominated in medieval times by the powerful Mortimer family.

Vaughan's Way: A waymarked trail between Kington and Bredwardine, linking Offa's Dyke Path with the Wye Valley Walk. It makes part of a triangular walk – from Bredwardine to Hay on Wye along the Wye Valley Walk and return along Offa's Dyke Path.

Three Choirs Way: a route linking the cities and cathedrals of Hereford, Gloucester and Worcester through countryside of hop-yards, vineyards and orchards.

Marches Way: an unofficial long-distance path between Chester and Cardiff. It passes through the county from the Mortimer Forest towards Leominster and Hereford before heading towards Abbey Dore.

Walking Festival

The annual Summer Walking Festival takes place in June with over 60 guided walks throughout the county. The programme caters for all ages and abilities. There is also a smaller Winter Walking Festival between Christmas and New Year. (enquiries to Queenswood Tourist Information Centre, ☎ 01568 797842 or queenswoodtic@herefordshire.gov.uk.)

1. Hereford and the South

The south of the county is dominated by the ancient cathedral city of Hereford, whose main historical artefact, the Mappa Mundi, draws visitors from all over the world and is a symbol of the city's municipal and ecclesiastical importance from medieval times onwards. However, modern Hereford does not feel like the major city it once was. Although the twentieth century saw a significant expansion of housing around its periphery and some redevelopment in the centre, much of the heart of the city would still be recognizable to residents and merchants of the nineteenth century. The result is that, for visitors, Hereford is a city you can wander around and enjoy in a day.

Opposite page: The Old House, Hereford
Left: River Wye

South of Hereford, the River Wye dominates the landscape and traverses a broad floodplain, which marks the northern edge of the Wye Valley Area of Outstanding Natural Beauty, on its way to the market town of Ross-on-Wye. Beyond, lies the start of the Wye Gorge, Goodrich with its castle and the honey-pot of Symonds Yat. To the west of the Wye is an area of rolling hills and secluded villages in the ancient Welsh enclave of Archenfield.

Hereford City and Environs

Hereford is set at the heart of this rural county and is its only city. It borders the **River Wye** and its name recalls its strategic positioning as a military crossing point (*here* = army). Now the river frontage and the old fifteenth century bridge over the Wye are quieter and somewhat sidelined by more recent

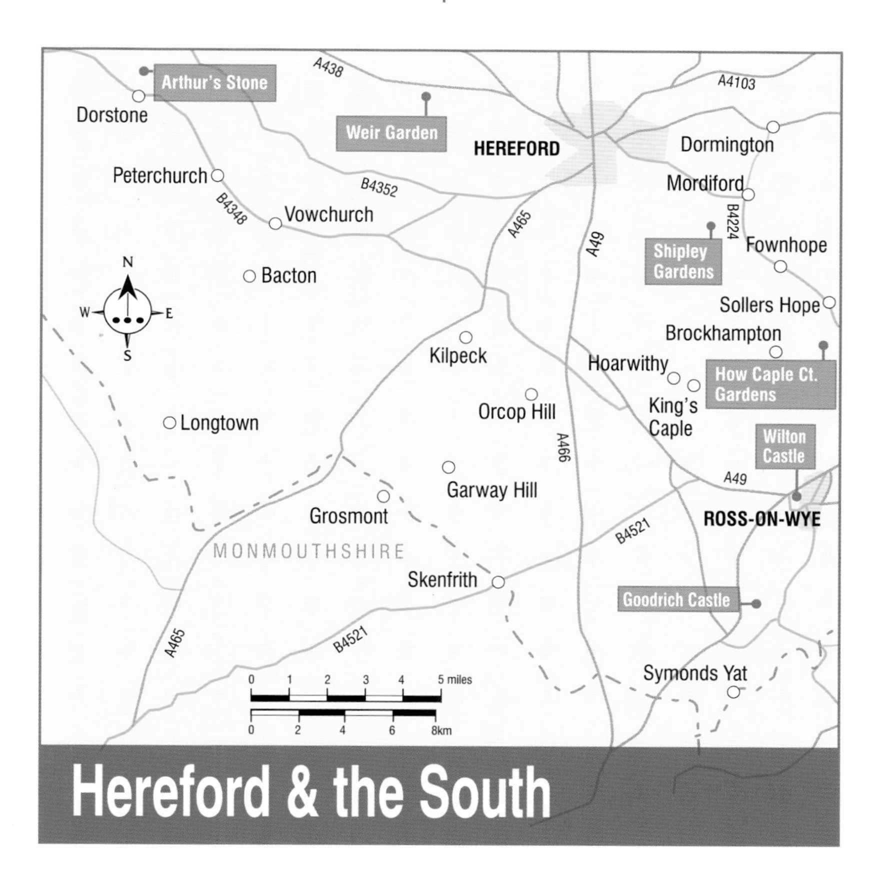

Hereford & the South

expansion and the modern road layout, which saw traffic diverted along the west side of the city and the pedestrianisation of the central area from St Peter's to All Saints churches.

The city centre has not entirely escaped the ravages of the civic development disasters of the 1970s and 1980s but significant parts or hints of the medieval walls, gates and streetscape have survived, along with some fine Georgian and Victorian buildings, though you often have to look to the upper storeys. It has its fair share of chain-stores and many of its independent shops are hanging on, as is its weekly central market in **High Town** on Wednesdays, though a far cry from the livestock and agricultural markets of yesteryear. The market used to dominate the whole of the main pedestrianised area but is now limited to the site outside the Victorian frontage of the **Butter Market**, an indoor trading area of stalls.

In the very centre of High Town, still standing amongst the modern shop fronts, are the striking black and white timbers of **The Old House**. The three gables of this delightful seventeenth century building are what remain of Butcher's Row, most of which was demolished in 1862, and can provide a welcome respite from the crowds of shoppers. The building was converted into a branch of the Worcester City and County Bank in 1882 before becoming a museum in 1928. Inside much of the interior has been intricately restored and it houses an extensive collection of oak furniture. There are even some 400 year old baby-walkers. Braille and audio guides are available. Admission is free.

North of High Town used to stand the Jewish Quarter with its synagogue, but most of it has been redeveloped with the red-brick horrors of Maylord Orchards shopping area, though a few timber-framed buildings still stand incongruously in various goods yards behind the shops on Maylord Street and Commercial Street. To the south the delightful medieval alleyway of **Church Street** leads past old shop-fronts and cafes, including the excellent Hereford Map Centre, to the Cathedral Close.

A little further away from the centre is **St. Peter's Square**, with its restored fourteenth century church, war memorial, and the neo-classical columns of the **Shire Hall** contrasting starkly with the unashamedly Victorian frontage of the **Town Hall** diagonally opposite. At the other end of High Town, at the top of Broad Street, rises the impressive spire of **All Saints Church**, every bit as worthy of exploration as the cathedral, and it too now has a cafe.

At the lower end of Broad Street is the **Tourist Information Centre** and opposite it is hard to miss the imposing west facade of **Hereford Cathedral,** which still dominates the area between the city centre and the River Wye. It is everything you would expect a cathedral to be in terms of religious architecture and antiquity but it is also a place that is reinvigorating itself in the twenty-first century. It has long been famous for the exhibition of the **Mappa Mundi**, a thirteenth century vellum map depicting the world with the city of Jerusalem at its centre, and the **Chained Library**, with its collection of rare printed books and 229 medieval manuscripts, including the eighth century Hereford

Gospels. There are helpful interpretative display boards and the staff are ever ready with further explanation.

The cathedral has recently celebrated the conclusion of three art projects and it is these which really help to bring the place to life. In the north transept the Shrine of St. Thomas has been refurbished with a reconstruction of a painted canopy – the reds, blues, and gold give a hint of the original medieval splendour of the place – and there are some modern textile hangings depicting the events in the saint's life. Nearby the story of St. Ethelbert has been celebrated with modern works and icons in wood and metal, while in the Audley Chapel four newly-commissioned stained-glass windows by artist Tom Denny commemorate the life of Thomas Treherne, the seventeenth century poet, priest and mystic. On their own these works of art would be good enough reason to visit, but combined with the building itself and the standing exhibitions you might find yourself spending more time here than you anticipated. There is also a good tearoom and some delightful gardens.

Opposite the cathedral on the south side of Broad Street, above the Library, is **Hereford Museum and Art Gallery**. Although housed in just two rooms, don't let outward appearances put you off. A spare half hour, or more, can easily be spent here. The museum tells the history of Herefordshire in a simple chronological sequence of small displays, from its geological past and period of prehistory through to modern times. The displays of implements, costumes and archaeological finds are mostly allowed to speak for themselves. There is even a huge stuffed sturgeon, which was caught in the River Wye in the nineteenth century. The Art Gallery mounts changing exhibitions of contemporary and local work. Admission to the museum is free.

On the western side of the city lies the **Cider Museum**, opposite the modern Bulmers cider plant. Inside you are taken on a walk-through guide of the traditional cider-making process, the varieties of apple and pear used, bottle-washing, pressing, storage, and distribution. There is a helpful reconstruction of a cider house with a number of presses, a coopers' area full of huge wooden vats and barrels, and a display of glass cider flutes. The Pomona Gallery contains some stunning watercolours of apple varieties and you can dial up interviews with former employees on old-fashioned telephones. They even distil their own cider liqueurs and brandy. A children's quiz is available and there is a cafe. For those wanting still more information on the history of cider there is an Archive Room available by appointment.

A little further west from the city centre, near Broomy Hill, tucked away just above the River Wye is the **Waterworks Museum** and it's a real treasure. Run by volunteers and enthusiasts from engineers to former doctors it gives a fascinating insight into the history of drinking water over the last 2000 years. Devotees come from far and wide to see the range of rescued and restored engines on site – there are ones worked by steam, gas, diesel, hot air, wind and water – but a good deal of effort and thought has been put into explaining and revealing the engineering to the non-expert.

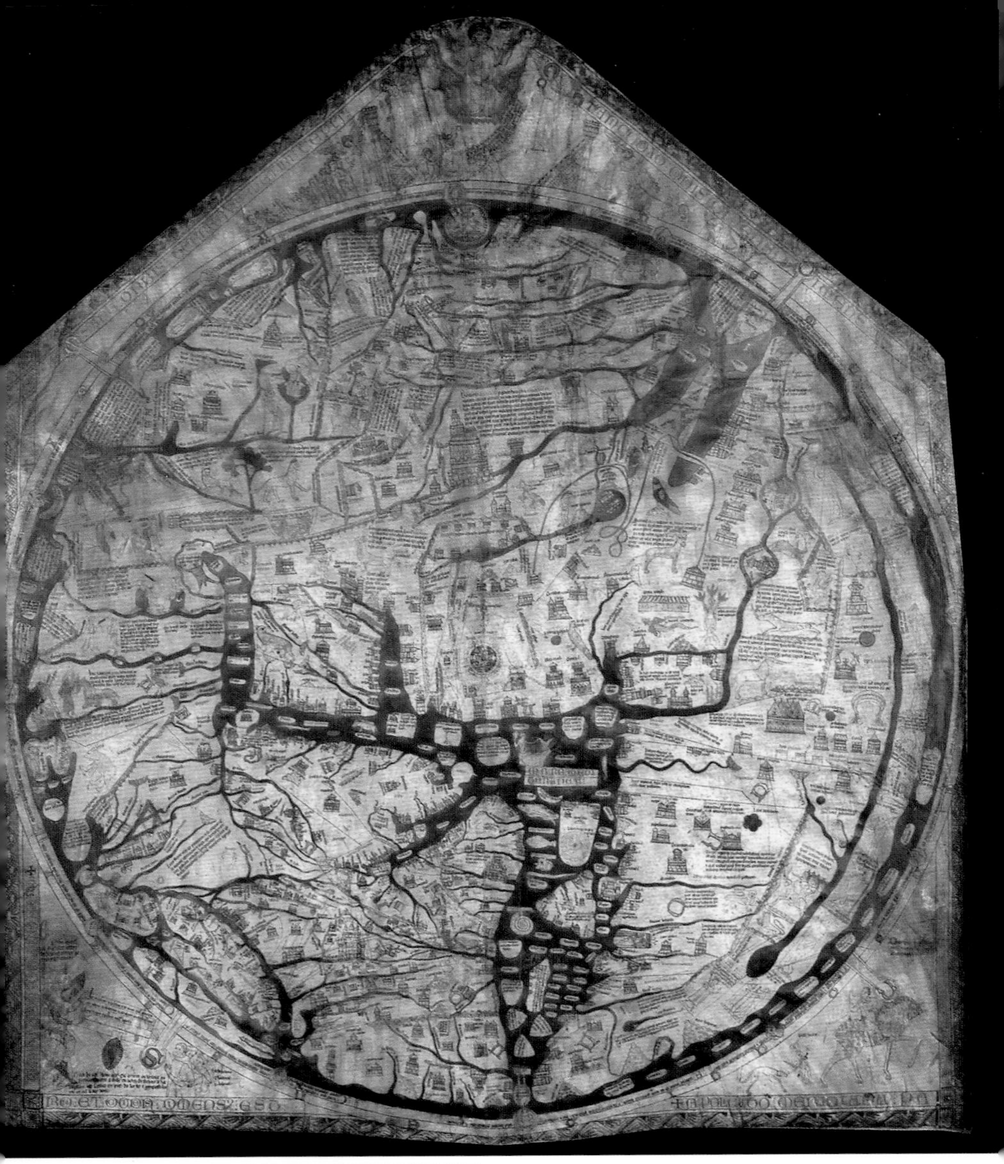

Above: The Mappa Mundi in Hereford Cathedral, the largest medieval map in existence, dating from c. 1300

Reproduced by kind permission of the Dean and Chapter of Hereford

Left: Hereford Cathedral

Waterworks Museum

Weir Garden

Many of the engines are fully operational and there are a number of hands-on devices to be pulled, pushed or turned. The buildings of the Victorian pumping station, themselves a scheduled ancient monument, house most of the engines, while recent grants have provided funds for newer areas and displays. If you have ever wondered just how it is that clean drinkable water comes out of the tap then this place will probably answer all of your queries, and more besides. Check for opening times, as they vary.

Easy to miss, a short walk beyond the city's former north gate along Widemarsh Street, is the unassuming red sandstone frontage of the **Coningsby Hospital and St. John Medieval Museum**. The oldest part of the buildings dates from the thirteenth century and, along with the nearby Victorian facades of the former grammar schools, forms a historical oasis amongst the traffic and some unfortunate twentieth century sheds and housing, but don't let this put you off. Inside is a delightful courtyard with almshouses on three sides, still occupied by Coningsby pensioners; the Custodian, Bill Raymond, lives at No. 2 and is most welcoming, knowledgeable and ready to guide visitors around. On the left are the former Coningsby Hospital and Chapel, named after Sir Thomas Coningsby who restored the buildings in the early seventeenth century to provide a refuge for worn-out soldiers and servants. Here you'll also find plenty of artefacts (including a grim skeleton) and information about Herefordshire's association with the Hospitaller Knights and the history of the ancient Order of St. John and its wars during the Crusades. To the rear of the almshouses is a real surprise – the ruins of a monastery of the Black Friars, established here by the Dominican Order of Preachers in the fourteenth century, and a rare and intact preaching cross. Check for afternoon opening times.

A little way out of Hereford (five miles west on the A438 towards Brecon) is **The Weir Garden**. Set into a steep bank stretching along the River Wye it offers an atmosphere of simple tranquility. The gardens are known for their spring and summer wildflowers, delightful among informal areas of planted woodland. Dotted here and there are a number of arresting features and plants and the whole scene attracts some varied wildlife. There is even what is thought to be the remains of a Roman nymphaeum. The staff are more than welcoming and it's astounding that the gardens are cared for by only two full-time gardeners and a small number of volunteers. It can be a real sun-trap, even in winter months, and a number of benches have been thoughtfully provided to help sit back and take in the vistas. Future projects include the restoration of the house's large Walled Garden, which lies a little way beyond the picnic tables away from the main gardens.

Towards Ross-on-Wye

Four miles south of Hereford, at the east end of the village of Holme Lacy, lie **Shipley Gardens**. Once bare fields, the owner Bob Macadie has, over four decades or more, brought a philosophical approach to his whimsical creation. The plantings have evolved through design and experiment into what is now a maturing landscape. One of the most surprising aspects of the gardens is the deliberate juxtaposition of trees and shrubs to create arresting vistas and contrasts. Dotted around are Bob's writings, which hint at the underlying concepts of the garden. Teas are served in the architecturally surprising glass-house. The website (shipleygardens.plus.com) is very useful.

Perched on a wooded hill above the River Wye just south of Fownhope is **Capler Camp**. The substantial earthworks of this Iron Age hill fort are a short walk from the viewpoint and picnic spot to its south. To reach the hill fort from the parking area on the minor road just follow the Wye Valley Walk northwards uphill. Of interest in the parking area is the **Brockhampton Bench** by artist David Jones, commissioned as part of the Village Artmakers project for Herefordshire. Carved from green oak in two parts the outer piece is curved to represent the looping River Wye, while the inner one portrays a map of the parish. The uprights are carved with images of local history, flora and fauna and one is inset with stained glass and ceramics

Brockhampton Church is a hidden gem. Not to be confused with the village and estate of the same name near Bromyard, it is one of only a few thatched churches in the country and forms part of the Brockhampton estate. It may come as a surprise that it was only built in 1901-2. Usually open, on display inside are two angel tapestries designed by Burne-Jones from the workshop of William Morris. With its immaculate lawns, trees and stone walls this secluded spot feels more like a private house and garden.

If churches are your bent, then you won't want to miss the extraordinary Italianate church at **Hoarwithy,** on the west bank of the River Wye, which boasts a Romanesque campanile for a tower and a cloister walk on the outside, with marbled and stained-glass treasures inside which would be commonplace in southern Italy but are unique in rural Herefordshire. On the high ground above the opposite bank of the Wye stands the village of **King's Caple**, which itself has an interesting church. This one occupies the former bailey of a Norman castle whose motte, known as Caple Tump, stands opposite. Some years ago in the churchyard near the cross a grim discovery was made of a plague pit, probably dating to the Black Death of 1348. The road leading into the village was once a Roman Road known as Caple Street and it passes the impressive red-brick King's Caple Court. The name of the house and village recall that local allegiance was once directly to the kings of England, rather than to the ecclesiastical authority of Hereford Cathedral.

How Caple Court Gardens, five miles north of Ross-on-Wye, form part of the home of the Lee family. Set on the slopes above the River Wye you can wander around the mature gardens, many of which are informal with dells and woodland to explore. A delightful place for children and picnics, there is even an open-air neoclassical theatre. The parish church stands in the grounds and is open to visitors. Inside are a Preedy stained glass window in the Gregory chapel, a restored sixteenth century diptych and some poignant plaques recording members of the Lee family. From the house you can follow footpaths down to the River Wye over horse paddocks and fields stocked with longhorn cattle. The Lee family also serves tea and ice-cream in the house's picturesque courtyard.

As 'Gate of the Wye' the market town of **Ross-on-Wye** has long been associated with the river that winds its way across the low ground to the north and west. The town itself stands on an outcrop of red sandstone – a good thing as there are still extensive floods, though the town has also long been known for its reliable climate and houses one of the oldest manual weather stations in the country. In the late eighteenth century the town became famous as the setting-off point for boating excursions down the river in what became known as the Wye Tour. The centre of Ross is still dominated by the red sandstone arches of the **Market Hall** which stands in a sloping triangular market place. On the Hall's upper storey there is now a heritage centre which houses exhibitions about the town's past. From here the town's streets radiate outwards – so far Ross has resisted the influx of endless chain stores and there are still a good number of independent local shops.

Above: John Kyrle, Ross-on-Wye and left two views of Ross

From miles around the skyline of Ross is dominated by the spire of **St. Mary's Church**. Situated at the highest point of the town, most of the building was completed in the thirteenth and fourteenth centuries and it has been much restored since. Inside is a profusion of tombs and memorials, notably those of the Rudhall family whose most famous member is William Rudhall, Attorney General to Henry VIII. This family also financed the erection of the former almshouses nearby. The churchyard cross is a grim record of the town's 315 plague victims of 1637 and stands close to the communal pit in which the bodies were buried.

Wherever you go in Ross there are memorials to the town's seventeenth century benefactor John Kyrle. His black and white timbered house stands opposite the Market Hall, St. Mary's Church also contains his monument and tomb, and next to the churchyard is **The Prospect**, a garden first laid out by John Kyrle in 1700 for the purpose of providing recreational walks and clean drinking water for the townsfolk. The pub on Wye Street is called The Man of Ross, the secondary school is named after him and there is even a John Kyrle Walk which covers a three mile circular route through the town and the river meadows to the west. A leaflet is available from the Tourist Information Centre at the top of the High Street.

However, if you want a breather from shopping or local history you can escape down Wye Street to the riverside gardens and some great views out over the meadows of the River Wye. There are lawns, benches and some eye-catching contemporary sculptures by the Polish sculptor Walenty Pytel. From here there is a short and pleasant walk by the river downstream to Wilton Bridge.

Here, just north of Ross-on-Wye on the north bank of the river guarding an old ford and the more modern bridge stands the restored ruins of **Wilton Castle**. The walls and fortifications date back to the Norman conquest but in more recent times the castle fell into disrepair. Now it has to a large extent been rescued by the current owners, Sue and Alan Parslow, in association with English Heritage. Although very much a family home, the gardens and grounds can be viewed on a number of Open Days (most Wednesdays and some Sundays, March – August). The restoration work took seven hard years and included the rebuilding of substantial parts of the walls and towers. You can trace the different periods of the castle from the Norman motte and bailey, the (now dry) moat, the inner ward with its fourteenth century towers, the remains of a Tudor Manor House, and the present house which dates from Georgian and Victorian times. Guided tours and private events can be arranged and it is also open in conjunction with the National Gardens Scheme. Standing in the south-facing gardens amongst the restored facades it is clear to see that this historic structure is now set for its thousandth anniversary, and beyond.

Goodrich Castle is rightly one of the best known attractions in the area. In 2007 a new Visitor Centre, cafe, and shop were built. It is a magnificent example of medieval castle-building and there is plenty to explore. A useful audio-guide is provided and there are information boards to help bring the ruins to life, as well as a leaflet for children. Look out for Roaring Meg, the deadly mortar, which was fired in anger at its walls during the Civil War, and the steps to the top of the Norman Keep are well worth tackling for the view from the roof. Special events run throughout the year and there is a useful information board on walks around nearby **Coppett Hill**. This is a local nature reserve and former common. Now it is an area of an open hillside of woods, steep bracken-covered slopes and farmland almost encircled by the River Wye. It is a great

Goodrich Castle

Cider

There is documentary evidence that cider has been made in Herefordshire since medieval times, and it is likely that it was established as a drink well before then. However, what could be called modern cider production seems to have started in the seventeenth century. It was then that one of the first modern agriculturalists, John Worlidge, published a revolutionary book called the *Vinetum Britannicum or, A Treatise of Cider and other Wines and Drinks,* which looked at farming in terms of an industry and advocated cider-making over wine-making, based on scientific observations and knowledge of climate and topography. Worlidge, and others of his time, laid the foundations for systematic agricultural practices which today we take for granted.

Traditionally many farms in the county would have had their own cider mill and press and would have produced cider for their own consumption and for farm labourers. It was even the case that cider would be provided as part of a worker's wages. Small-scale cider-making was a relatively straight-forward process, especially compared to wine production. You can still see old troughs and millstones in farmyards, though presses are rarer. The cider apples were harvested in autumn, washed, and then crushed in a circular trough by an upright millstone, driven round by a horse. An apple holds a surprising amount of juice, up to three-quarters or more of its weight, and this was fed into barrels for fermenting, while the remaining pulp was stacked in cloths on a press to make a 'cheese'. Here, wooden boards were screwed down to extract any remaining juice. The remnant of the pulp, called pomace, was then used as extra feed for livestock.

In the second half of the nineteenth century the Woolhope Naturalists' Field Club undertook to record and produce illustrations of over 400 apples and pears in what has become known as the *Herefordshire Pomona*. The publication of the *Pomona* accompanied a boom in large-scale cider production in Herefordshire and many of the well-known cider families opened factories at this time, including Westons in 1880, based in the village of Much Marcle, and Bulmers of Hereford in 1887, now the world's largest cider maker. The late twentieth century has seen something of a resurgence of interest in cider and in recent years many small cider producers have once again started making their own cider and perry on farms, though now using modern production techniques.

For those wanting to explore all aspects of Herefordshire cider making, traditional and modern, the Cider Museum in Hereford is a good place to start. There is also an official Cider Route around the county – a leaflet is available from tourist information centres or the website www.ciderroute.co.uk. There are also a number of events and festivals, including the International Cider and Perry Competition, in May, and the Cider Making Festival, in October. Both are held at the Hereford Cider Museum.

place for exploring and nature-watching – look out especially for butterflies and the huge outcrops of puddingstone on its northern end, while its southern ridge leads down to the River Wye and the base of the famous Coldwell Rocks on whose lofty cliff faces peregrine falcons have their nests.

The riverside honey-pot of **Symonds Yat** is likewise well known. Here the River Wye enters a section of gorge, with dramatic limestone cliffs towering above the hotels, bars, canoe centre, cycle hire cabin and river-cruise boats. On a sunny day there is just a hint of something more exotic beyond the crowds but it is easy to escape on the trails, on foot or bike, along the river or up into the woods. On the slopes above **Symonds Yat (East)**, which is just over the border into Gloucestershire, there is a viewpoint for the peregrines that nest among Coldwell Rocks and in summer you may well also hear the calls and clunking of climbers and their gear on the high limestone outcrops, while back down below a hand-pull ferry provides a nostalgic way of crossing to the west side of the river and back into Herefordshire at **Symonds Yat (West)**. Here by way of access from the A40 there is Jubilee Park and, if you are looking for something to entertain young children, it could be worth a detour to the **Amazing Hedge Puzzle and Butterfly Zoo**.

Into Archenfield

To the southwest of Hereford, and reaching southwards into Monmouthshire, is an area of rolling hills and river valleys traditionally known as **Archenfield**. Bounded on the north by the Worm Brook and in the east by the River Wye, to the west it stretches to the slopes of the Black Mountains. The ancient name for the area is Ergyng, which itself may be derived from the name of the Roman settlement of Ariconium at Weston under Penyard near Ross-on-Wye. For centuries the area was essentially a Welsh enclave within the county of Herefordshire, with the Welsh language spoken here by many locals well into the eighteenth century, testament to which is the number of places still with Welsh names. Hidden among its maze of narrow, winding lanes is a collection of scenic hamlets and villages.

One of the best known and most visited is the ancient settlement of **Kilpeck.** It lies on higher ground above what was once the strategic route from Hereford into Wales and which now carries the A465 Hereford to Abergavenny road. Most striking is the **church of St. Mary and St. David**. The semi-circular apse at the east end is a sign of its Norman origins and apart from some recent restoration work the building has remained largely unchanged since it was constructed in the twelfth century. People come specifically to see the south porch and the eighty-five grotesque motifs whose carvings extend on the corbel table all the way round the church – there are figures of birds, monsters, dragons and human forms in various risque poses, with a number of gaps marking Victorian attempts to remove ones which were thought just too bawdy. Behind the church lie the ruins of a Norman motte and bailey **castle**, which itself probably replaced an existing structure. Around both buildings runs what is thought to be the outline of

Ferry at Symonds Yat

a Saxon stockade and you can clearly see its northern edge above the slopes of the valley, giving a great vantage point to the north and west to the Black Mountains. The main village lies to the south of the church and castle; the school and village shop are now closed but the pub, the Kilpeck Inn, has recently been given a new lease of life.

A little to the south, hidden among the folds and meadows of the Garren valley, is **Orcop Hill,** one of the highest points on a chain of hills between the valleys of the River Monnow, to the south, and the Worm Brook, to the north. It is sited in often by-passed countryside, equidistant from Hereford, Ross and Monmouth eleven miles away. This scattered settlement, which stretches south to **Orcop** village, used to boast five pubs. Now, only The Fountain remains. This pub traces its name to the nearby Copywell (or Coppice Well) and until the 1960s it was the main source of water in the area, requiring the inhabitants of the Garren Valley to ferry their water for considerable distances. Now it is a great area for walking and you can explore for miles in almost complete solitude, with only the views to distract you.

Moving towards the county border, the open slopes of **Garway Hill** above the Monnow Valley provide some higher level walking. You can reputedly see seven counties from here on a clear day. Wild horses survive on this upland common all year round, getting their water from nearby Black Pool, which not only mysteriously lasts all year with no visible spring but also provides a breeding ground for the rare and protected great-crested newt. The hill is a haven for wildlife, has never been ploughed and there are said to be over seventy species of bird, including skylark, song thrush and yellowhammer and it's a great habitat for butterflies. A little to the southeast is the village of **Garway**, high above the Monnow Valley, which boasts the church of St. Michael whose round nave is a copy of the Holy Sepulchre in Jerusalem.

Just over the border into Monmouthshire, but not to be missed while in this part of the county, are the historic villages of **Skenfrith** and **Grosmont** in the secluded Monnow Valley. Clustered round a bend of the River Monnow the village of **Skenfrith**, with its church and castle, one of the so-called trilateral castles, provides a picturesque setting of modern rural life. People are free to wander among the ruins and fortifications, which date to the eleventh century. At the castle's far end are the remains of an old water mill and the recent rediscovery of the medieval quay has also pointed to the importance of the river as a means of transporting goods from Monmouth and beyond. It is likely that flat-bottomed barges would have been used, hauled up-river by horses or gangs of men in harness – now villagers and visitors merely cool off in the Monnow's waters on hot summer days. Parking is available on what was once the stone-revetted moat of the medieval castle, and there are a number of information boards to help with exploration. There is a plush pub, The Bell, and even a community shop, staffed by volunteers at weekends ever-ready to supply tea and ice cream. A few miles up the valley lies **Grosmont**, and the second of the trilateral castles (the third is White Castle to the southwest). Completely different in character, the village and castle stand on a steep-sided hill high above the Monnow Valley. It is still possible to climb to the top of some of the castle's battlements and explore the now dry moat. The village is thriving and still has a post office and the delightful Gentle Jane's tearoom.

Garway Hill

Places to Visit

The Old House

High Town, HR1 2AA
☎ 01432 260694
herefordmuseums@herefordshire.gov.uk
Well preserved example of a 17th century timber-framed building in the heart of Hereford
Open all year: Tue-Sat 10–5, also Sun and Bank Hol Mon 10-4 Apr-Sep.
Closed: Mon, Good Fri, 25-26 Dec, 1 Jan.
Admission free
Location: city centre

Hereford Cathedral

Cathedral Close, HR1 2NG
☎ 01432 374202
www.herefordcathedral.org
visits@herefordcathedral.org
Mappa Mundi exhibition, Chained Library, cafe, shop
Open: Summer (Easter to Oct) Mon-Sat: 10-5; Winter (Nov to Easter) Mon-Sat: 10-4; Sunday opening times vary
Exhibition, shop and café are closed on Good Fri, 25-27 Dec,1 Jan.
Guided Tours: Summer only, Mon-Sat: 11.15am and 2.15pm
Garden Tours: June-Aug, Wed and Sat: 2.30pm
Location: city centre

Hereford Museum and Art Gallery

Broad Street, HR4 9AU
☎ 01432 260692
herefordmuseums@herefordshire.gov.uk
Open: All year, Tue-Sat 10–5; Apr-Sep, Sun and Bank Holiday Mon 10-4
Closed: Mon, Good Fri, 25-26 Dec, 1 Jan.
Admission free
Location: city centre

Waterworks Museum

Broomy Hill, HR4 0LJ
☎ 01432 357236
www.waterworksmuseum.org.uk
The museum traces the history of drinking water from cave-dwellers up to the present day through working engines, display panels, illuminated displays, guidebooks and films.
Open: Tue 11-4 all year (except two weeks at Christmas and New Year)
Location: ¾ mile west of city centre (can be reached by Riverside Walk)

Coningsby Hospital and St. John Medieval Museum

Widemarsh Street, HR4 9HN
☎ 01432 358134 (The Custodian)
Home of crusaders of the Order of St. John and an ex-serviceman's hospital and chapel; museum explains the links between the Crusades, the Knights Templar and The Hospitaller Knights; site of The Blackfriars Monastery.
Open: Wed-Sat 11-3 (Easter to Oct)
Location: north of city centre

The Weir Garden

Swainshill, HR4 7QF
☎ 01981 590509
www.nationaltrust.org.uk
theweir@nationaltrust.org.uk
Informal 1920s riverside garden with fine views created by Roger Parr with views towards the River Wye and Black Mountains.

Open: late Jan 11–4 (Sat, Sun); Feb 11–4 (Wed-Sun); Mar-Apr 11-5 (daily); May-Nov 11–5 (Wed-Sun); also Bank Holiday Mon.
Location: 5 miles west of Hereford on A438

Towards Ross-on-Wye

Shipley Gardens

Holme Lacy, HR2 6LS
☎ 01432 870356
www.herefordshiregardens.co.uk
30 acres of mixed environmental habitats adjacent to the River Wye
Tea rooms, gift shop, plant sales.
Open: every day from end Mar-end of Oct, 10-6.
Location: 5 miles SE of Hereford on B4399, on eastern edge of Holme Lacy

How Caple Court Gardens

How Caple, HR1 4SX
☎ 01989 740611
www.howcaplecourt.co.uk
info@howcaple.co.uk
11 acre gardens dating from Edwardian times above River Wye with extensive views (house not open to the public); coaches and parties welcome.
Courtyard tearoom, Stable shop
Open: 10-5 daily, mid Mar-mid Oct.
Location: 5 miles north of Ross-on-Wye near village of How Caple

Wilton Castle

Wilton, Ross-on Wye, HR9 5JA
☎ 01989 565759
www.wiltoncastle.eclipse.co.uk
sue@wiltoncastle.co.uk
Ruins of a restored 12th century castle and 2 acre gardens on the banks of the River Wye.
Open: most Weds and some Suns, Mar-Aug (check for exact dates)
Location: off Wilton roundabout on A40, ½ mile west of Ross

Goodrich Castle

Goodrich, HR9 6HY
☎ 01600 890538
www.english-heritage.org.uk
11th century castle on wooded hill above the River Wye and picturesque valley of Symonds Yat.
Visitor centre, cafe, shop
Open: Jan-Feb 10-4 (Wed-Sun); Mar 10-5 (Wed-Sun); Apr-Jun 10-5 (daily); Jul-Aug 10-6 (daily); Sep-Oct 10-5 (daily); Nov-Dec 10-4 (Wed-Sun).
Closed: 24-26 Dec, 1 Jan
Location: Goodrich Village, 5 miles S of Ross-on-Wye off A40

Wye Valley Butterly Zoo

Symonds Yat (West), HR9 6DA
☎ 01600 890360
www.butterflyzoo.co.uk
Open: daily 10-5
Location: Between Ross-on-Wye and Monmouth, off A40 towards Symonds Yat (West)

The Amazing Hedge Puzzle

Symonds Yat (West), HR9 6DA
☎ 01600 890360
www.mazes.co.uk
Open: daily from 11
Location: Between Ross-on-Wye and Monmouth, off A40 towards Symonds Yat (West)

2 Ledbury, Bromyard and the East

The east of the county has two market towns, Ledbury, in the Leadon Valley, and Bromyard, which stands on the River Frome. Both are delightful places from which to explore the surrounding countryside, which is still dominated by apple orchards, vineyards and hop-growing. It is also good walking country, with the Woolhope Dome to the east of Hereford, the Malvern Hills near Ledbury, and Bromyard offering the Downs and Bringsty Common right on its doorstep. For those wanting to visit historic houses the area has old manor houses at Hellens, near Much Marcle, and the moated house at Lower Brockhampton on the large Brockhampton Estate. For castles, Eastnor Castle, near Ledbury, is one of the country's finest fairytale creations. In addition, there are plenty of villages offering pubs and walks and churches to visit.

Opposite page: Woolhope Dome
Left: Millennium Clock, Bromyard

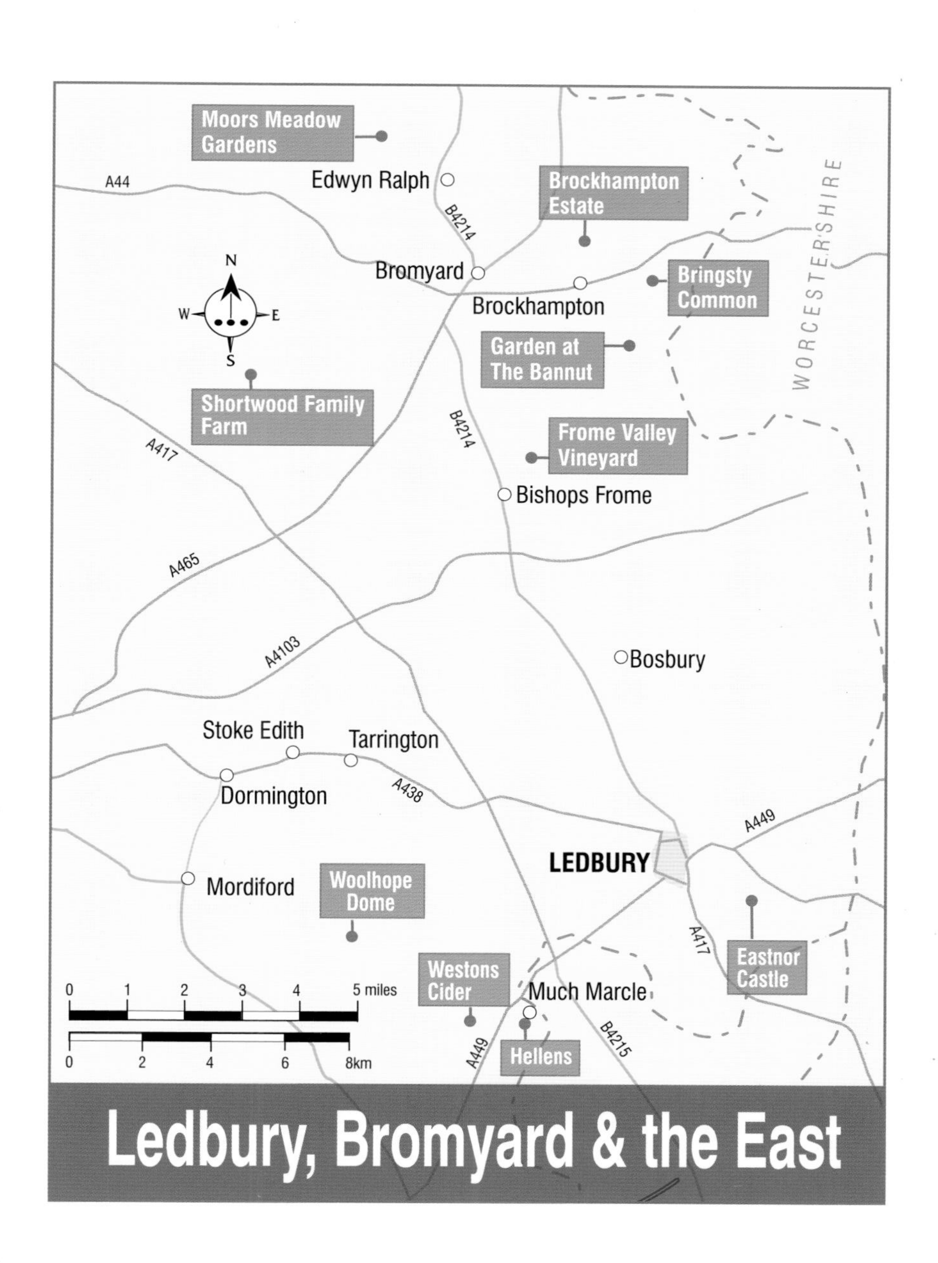

Ledbury, Bromyard & the East

The Woolhope Dome

To the east of Hereford, rising sharply from the valley of the River Wye to a height of over 250 metres, is a substantial area of hills known as the **Woolhope Dome**. Of geological and botanical importance the Dome has drawn naturalists and geologists from all over the world. Here, the underlying rock of Silurian limestone, some 400 million years old, contrasts with the Old Red Sandstone found in much of the nearby Wye river valley and gives rise to the paler soils underfoot as well as the variety of woodland, wild-flower meadows and extensive hedgerows. It also gave its name to The Woolhope Club. Founded in 1851 as the Woolhope Naturalists' Field Club, its interests now cover the local history, archaeology, and architecture of Herefordshire, as well as natural history and geology; its headquarters and Club Library are in the Woolhope Room in Hereford Library.

Haugh Wood occupies the centre of the Dome and, along with **Broadmoor Common,** provides scenic walking over undulating fields and through woods rich in flora and fauna. The main village in the centre is **Woolhope**, known as the Walled Village because of its plethora of limestone walls. It also has a good pub and a church, famous for its medieval coffin lids. From here it is easy to walk or drive to **Marcle Ridge** at Hooper's Oak. The way along the ridge here has been in use as a travellers' route since at least the Bronze Age and there are extensive views north-eastwards to the Malvern Hills and south-eastwards to the Cotswolds. There is a car park where the road divides just short of the highest point on the ridge.

Clustered around the Dome's rim are a collection of picture-postcard villages. **Mordiford**, situated on the western edge, is worth seeing for its bridge, which dates back to the fourteenth century and is one of the oldest bridges in Herefordshire. Before then the crossing of the River Lugg was by way of an ancient ford. A little above the bridge is the confluence of the River Frome and a few hundred metres below the Lugg joins the Wye. From the bridge the impressive red-brick rectory can be seen and nearby is the church, dedicated to the Holy Rood, which dates in origin from Norman times and contains a Record of Occurrence of 27th May 1811, recording the details of a catastrophic flood of the Pentaloe Brook, which flows into the Lugg just below the bridge.

Tucked away in the southern folds is the tranquil settlement of **Sollers Hope**. It is worth a detour here to see the ornamental chimney stacks of Court Farm, a fifteenth century manor house, and the church which dates from earlier still, itself the restoration of a Saxon building, and was financed by the brother of Dick Whittington, the famous Mayor of London. Easy to miss to the north of the churchyard is a curious tump, a mound reputedly marking the remains of a Romano-British camp.

Ringing the Dome to the north on the A438 to Ledbury are the three villages of **Dormington**, which gives a good walk up Backbury Hill with its legendary St. Ethelbert's Camp, **Stoke**

Edith, where there is a well named, like the village, after the daughter of King Edgar, and **Tarrington,** with a pub, the Tarrington Arms, and an ancient yew tree and preaching cross with a fourteenth century base in its churchyard.

The eastern side of the dome slopes more gently towards Ledbury. Here, just off the A417, in origin a Roman road, are a number of scattered hamlets set amongst fields, which were former hopyards and apple orchards. The tiny church of **Aylton** has an old sundial and nearby there is a five hundred year old Manorial Barn currently undergoing restoration. **Putley** likewise has timber-framed houses and another small church, built on the site of a Roman villa. The whole area is good for taking a stroll or cycling and seeing just what you come across.

Just off the A449 towards Ross-on-Wye lies the more substantial village of **Much Marcle**. Here you will find what has been called 'the jewel in the crown of Herefordshire Homes' and if there is one historic house in the county you visit, then let it be **Hellens**. This Manor reaches back in origin to the eleventh century and the foundations of the house's east walls date to the period of the signing of the Magna Carta. The main parts of the house in existence today were built in the fourteenth to the seventeenth centuries and over time it has been owned by a number of prestigious families including the de Baluns, the de Helyons, who gave their name to the place, the Mortimers and the Walwyns.

More recently the house has passed into the Munthe family, at the marriage of the philanthropist and physician Axel Munthe, of *The Story of San Michele* fame. Outside and inside there are surprises and delights round every corner. In the grounds there are a rare seventeenth century octagonal dovecote, and an old Cider Mill House with a working press. This is used to make their own cider as part of the Big Apple cider festival every October. There are also restored sixteenth century barns in which are regularly held concerts, arts workshops, and literary events. Inside you are taken on a guided tour starting with the Stone Hall, a medieval half-timbered hall with a minstrel's gallery used also as a courtroom; next come the day rooms with a wealth of furniture and heirlooms and paintings by, amongst others, Reynolds, Van Dyck, Hogarth, Goya, Gainsborough, Lely, Gennari, and Tintoretto; upstairs of particular note are the Cordoba Room, which is lined throughout with tooled eighteenth century leather, and Hetty's Room, with its sad story of abandoned elopement plaintively etched out on one of the window panes. Throughout there is a real sense of a house which continues to be lived in and cherished, not just for its long historical associations but also for what it can best foster today.

The **Church of St. Bartholomew** in the village of Much Marcle is well worth a visit. The building is of considerable archaeological interest itself and it contains some of the finest effigies of any church in the county, including a rare oak figure of a man in medieval dress, putatively identified with Walter de Helyon who lived at Hellens in the fourteenth century. Outside is a

Above: Weston's Cider Mill

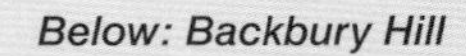

Below: Backbury Hill

Above: Church Lane, Ledbury

The Dovecote and Cider Mill at Hellens Manor

famous hollow yew tree, thought to be at least one thousand years old, and in its hollow interior you can even take a rest on some wooden seating.

Just west off the A449 is **Westons Cider**. The family has been making cider and perry commercially for well over a hundred years and they have now expanded their business to include tours around the cider mill to show the various stages of cider-making, at the end of which the different blends of cider can be tasted. For children there are also animals to be seen in the Farm Park and a play area. There are various events held throughout the year and there is also a cafe.

Around Ledbury

The ancient market town of **Ledbury** stands in the Leadon Valley against a backdrop of wooded hills. It is best known for its black and white timber-framed buildings, the Talbot and the Feathers Hotels, along with the Market House which still dominates the centre of the town, set prominently on its pillars of chestnut taken from Malvern Chase some four hundred years ago. Now it is still a busy market town and, despite the traffic, which can still dominate, there is a certain charm in its obvious medieval origins, the variety of its clustered architecture and the fact that the place is still operating as a centre for local trade and commerce. There are a number of interesting independent shops, including two local bookshops with full sections on local history.

Ledbury itself claims association with a number of poets. Elizabeth Barrett Browning spent her childhood nearby, at Hope End and is commemorated in the name of the town's library. The poet laureate John Masefield is now most prominently commemorated in the name of the local high school. The American poet Robert Frost lived in the town for a short while and, along with other 'Dymock Poets' Rupert Brooke and Edward Thomas, found inspiration for writing in the surrounding country. The village of **Dymock** itself lies a few miles to the south, just over the border into Gloucestershire. From here Dymock aficionados can retrace the poets' footsteps on a number of trails through Dymock Woods and up May Hill. A more tenuous link is claimed to William Langland, of *Piers Plowman* fame, but precious little is actually known about this fourteenth century writer. The **Ledbury Poetry Festival** was started in 1997 and has become internationally renowned. The actual festival takes place in the summer, but there is also a year round series of community activities and events.

For a taste of more down to earth local artistry, try the wall paintings in the **16th Century Painted Room** in the Town Council Offices in **Church Lane**, an attractive cobbled street leading away from the Market House. Here in the offices in 1988 during routine restoration work the discovery was made in one of the first floor rooms of decorative pictures and patterns painted onto the wattle-and-daub in-fill between the timbers. Quatrefoils with leaves, fruit and flowers, as well as handwritten text, were uncovered. Though clearly amateur in execution the finished result is charming.

A little further along Church Lane is the **Butcher Row Museum**. Although small, for those interested in the details of Victorian life, the room contains a range of artefacts. However, this medieval alley leaves its best to last.

Standing on higher ground above the centre of the town is the **church of St. Michael and All Angels**. The site is an ancient one and there was a large pre-Conquest church here long before the Normans arrived. No one knows exactly why the detached tower was built but it makes for a notable and impressive curiosity. Inside, in addition to the scale of the place, the Decorated windows and the strange port-hole windows, the building is full of memorials, to both the high and low-born. On the south side of the nave William Miles' monument records his career as a businessman in Bristol and the West Indies. It was erected by his only surviving son, six other children all predeceasing their father. The nave floor is covered with memorial stones, which make a patchwork of the local history of the town's tradespeople, plumbers, pinmakers, chandlers, mercers and benefactors. In the central aisle is a memorial to the Mutlow family, whose four children all died in early infancy between 1813 and 1825.

If walking and cycling are on the agenda, there are guided walks around the town and a signed cycle route, the Ledbury Loop, which takes in Dymock and Eastnor. Lying to the east of Ledbury are the **Malvern Hills**, which form part of the larger Malvern Hills Area of Outstanding Natural Beauty (AONB). Designated in 1959 this area extends into Worcestershire and Gloucestershire and is rich in geology, history and wildlife. Within easy reach of Ledbury is the car park on the A449, just below the Herefordshire Beacon. Rising to over 1000ft, this is the site of Iron Age earthworks, known as the British Camp, and from here there are great views over the Cotswolds to the east and the Black Mountains west into Wales. It is also a good starting point for walks along the ridge itself, either northwards to the Worcestershire Beacon or to Midsummer Hill near the southern end. For cycling, the AONB has produced a leaflet, *By Bike in the Foothills of the Malverns*, which outlines four routes exploring the landscape, culture and heritage of the area.

One of the best known buildings near Ledbury is **Eastnor Castle**. It stands east of the town, just off the A438 Tewkesbury road near the village of Eastnor. Famous as something of a fairytale castle its style is part Norman fortification, part Italian palazzo, and part Regency country house. Built to impress by the 1st Earl Somers in the early nineteenth century – its construction took fourteen years at a whopping cost then of £85,000 – the scale of the undertaking is truly massive and certainly conveys a sense of power and prestige which many ruined castles now fail to produce, though whether it succeeds as a piece of architecture in its own right is contentious. The House is still, in part, a family home but many of the rooms are open to the public gaze. Their collections are truly catholic: Gothic arches, early English furniture, faux medieval tapestries, classical antiquities from Mesopotamia, Victorian furnishings and paintings, Sienese

Above: The Painted Room, Ledbury

bookcases, pieces of Louis XVI, Pugin interiors, family portraits and works by modern British artists, hand-painted Chinese wallpaper, and even a pig-tail of human hair on a Mandarin's hat. In short, expect the unexpected. If dizzied by the unfathomable eclecticness of it all, there are grounds to wander in, which include more prosaic items such as trees, terraces, tearooms, a maze, a children's playground and plenty of lawns for picnics or regaining a sense of equilibrium. The grounds too, throughout the year, are host to a wide range of special events, including fairs, rallies, concerts, and festivals.

Between Ledbury and Bromyard

Further up the Leadon valley off the B4214 is the village of **Bosbury** and it is well worth detouring here en route, if only to see another village of black and white timbered houses. The area round about used to be one of the largest hop growing regions of England outside Kent in its heyday of the eighteenth and nineteenth centuries. **Bosbury Church** is perhaps best known for having one of the county's seven detached bell towers. This one has its bells still, six of them, the oldest of which dates back to the seventeenth century, and a nineteenth century clock. The walls of the tower are impressive and may indicate that the main purpose of the tower was as a refuge against incursions by the Welsh in the thirteenth century, when the tower was originally built. The church itself is also made of red sandstone but is thought to date in its earliest foundation to Saxon times. Inside are four memorials to women, a saint, a novelist, a benefactor, and an organ donor. There is also a Jacobean pulpit. The village itself is a delight to wander through and the pub, The Bell, is still very much at the heart of the place. Dating from the fifteenth century, the building, originally two houses, was owned by the Bishops of Hereford, though it only became a pub in the late nineteenth century. The village is also famous for an actual bell, a large bronze one, possibly Celtic, which was dug up in a nearby field in 1890.

Running between Ledbury and Bromyard is the valley of the **River Frome**, which traces a course south-westwards to join the River Lugg east of Hereford. The valley has been instrumental for local agriculture and the growing of hops, apples, and now wine. The delightful village of **Bishop's Frome** lies on the river, south of Bromyard on the B4214, surrounded on three sides by hills. Its **church of St. Mary's** has a famous chalice-shaped font, a large Breccia or cornstone which is one of eight in the county, some medieval paintings, the effigy of a knight, and a notable lychgate. The village now has two pubs, a number much reduced from the time when it used to attract hundreds of seasonal farm workers. North of the village, at Paunton Court, lie the **Frome Valley Vineyards**, which are open to visitors who wish to see the vineyards and sample the white wines produced here. To the south is the **Hop Pocket Craft Centre** which houses various gift shops and eateries in what used to be large lime kilns.

Below: Eastnor Castle © Nigel Harriman

Around Bromyard

Tucked away in the north-east corner of the county in the upper Frome valley is the small market town of **Bromyard**. Quieter now that the A44 by-passes the town on its southern edge, the main thoroughfare of Broad Street has along its length Georgian and Victorian shopfronts, interspersed with older timber-framed buildings, which mark out the town's considerable history. The surrounding area has long been known for its hop-growing, though the fields of hop poles have long since been replaced by modern growing methods using strings. However, the landscape is predominantly rural and farming still dominates. Part of Bromyard's charm lies in its understated simplicity. The **Market Square** lies at the eastern end of Broad Street, small and picturesque with many of the buildings concealing the timber frames of four hundred year old houses. Above the gallery on the south side is the Millennium Clock, which performs a bawdy routine on the hour. Here also is the **Dr. Who Time Machine Museum**, which houses a collection of models and toys from television, film and science fiction.

From here, Broad Street leads into the High Street, with its shops and pubs. Rowberry Street contains the surviving parts of a number of Tudor, and possibly older, buildings, while Church Street leads to the cross-shaped **St. Peter's Church**. St. Peter himself, with his keys can be seen carved above the southern doorway. It is possible that this carving was originally set into an older building, but no trace remains of the Saxon 'monasterium', which documents record as existing in the ninth century. Of particular interest and unusualness is the exterior stair turret on the outside of the tower, complete with the castellation at the top and inside there are a number of fourteenth century tomb recesses.

East of the town are two areas of delightful walking country. **Bromyard Downs** rise steeply above the River Frome and cover an area of almost three hundred acres. Paths criss-cross this former common and it is still open to all to enjoy. A little further along the A44 is **Bringsty Common**, a slightly smaller area of rolling grassland, scrub and wooded streams. There are paths, bridleways and by-ways. It was also a favourite haunt of the composer Edward Elgar, who used to meet the writer George Bernard Shaw here for their lengthy strolls. Now people come to walk the dog or for a short wander. There is plenty of wildlife on offer, with over thirty species of butterfly recorded, and autumn brings a display of fungi varieties. You might even glimpse an elusive falcon, the hobby.

In between the Bromyard Downs and Bringsty Common lie two contrasting places to visit, one small, one large. **The Garden at the Bannut**, on the south side of the A44 two miles east of Bromyard, is a small 3ac/1.2ha garden, which has evolved over the last twenty-five years since its owners used the place as a nursery for growing heathers. The area to the front is still planted out for heathers but the rest of the garden has been created from what was largely once pasture. It is a real gardener's garden, with colour at most times of the year. There is a variety of different areas, including a Knot Garden planted entirely with heathers, Sink Gardens with alpine plants, a South Garden of mixed borders, shrubs and herbaceous plants, and an Old Goat Paddock with many interesting trees and a great viewpoint to the Malvern Hills. Dotted around are some intriguing sculptures and artifacts; and their tearoom has been highly commended by the Flavours of Herefordshire panel of judges.

In complete contrast, across the road, and a little nearer Bromyard, is **Brockhampton Estate**. Made up of five farms and hundreds of acres of mixed woodland, the estate has been managed by the National Trust for over fifty years. In the valley are streams, orchards and meadows, while the higher ground gives views to the Cotswolds, Malvern Hills and the Brecon Beacons. There are three car parks, each serving an area of the estate. The **Upper Estate car park** and the **Hollybank car park**, with its tearoom, are the setting-off points for the series of woodland and meadow walks of one to four miles. Along the routes there are oak trees planted over 500 years ago, the Lawn Pool, which was created as a landscape feature for the private Brockhampton House and as a draw for wildlife, and a wetland area once used to grow willow trees, as well as sculptures and the remains of two apple presses.

A mile further down the hill along the estate road lies **Lower Brockhampton**, a timber-framed manor house which dates back, in parts, to the fourteenth century. Over the moat stands a sixteenth century gatehouse, much restored in recent years. The main room in the house is the Great Hall and the whole has been furnished in the style of a medieval manor house, with other rooms given over to explaining some historical aspects of the estate. In sunny weather it is a tranquil place to relax, have a picnic or watch the Herefordshire cattle grazing in the surrounding fields.

To the north of Bromyard lies the roadside village of **Edwyn Ralph** and just off the B4214, before the actual village, is the church of St. Michael and All Angels. Built of local sandstone and roofed in clay tiles it stands near a motte and bailey castle, around which is thought to be the site of the former medieval village, most likely abandoned after the Black Death. Inside, among a wealth of memorials, is a collection of thirteenth and fourteenth century stone effigies. A number of the figures are depicted with legs crossed resting on a dog or lion. There is also a pardon monument of Maud de Edefin – say a prayer for her and receive a pardon of thirty days from the Lord Bishop of Worcester, and sixty from the Bishop of Hereford.

A couple of miles further along the B4214 towards Tenbury Wells is **Moors Meadow Garden**. It is an intriguing and eclectic garden, full of appeal to the general gardener as well as the true plantsman. Set on an open hillside overlooking the Kyre Valley, the plantings have evolved over the last fifty years. Amongst the unusual and the exotic there are seats and sculptures ingeniously fashioned from old farm implements and pieces of scrap metal. There is no set route to follow but there are plenty of surprises and hidden areas to explore and investigate. The mix and informality of the setting and design attracts wildlife, and added to this is the sense that the site has a long history of occupancy. There is also a small nursery, stocked with plants propagated from the gardens, so if a plant takes your fancy, you may well be able to take one home.

If you are looking to entertain children in this part of the county, **Shortwood Family Farm** may provide an answer. Sign-posted from the A417 to the south-west of Bromyard and from the town itself, it lies near the village of Pencombe among a maze of lanes and fields. Shortwood is a working dairy farm, owned by the Legge family since the beginning of the last century. Just over twenty years ago they started their family tours around the farm and this aspect has now grown into a major part of the business. The main emphasis for children, and adults, is a hands-on approach, where the animals can be seen at close quarters and the workings of a proper farm can be experienced, muck and all, so it might be an idea to bring wellies. There are goats, calves, donkeys, ducks, geese, pigs, chicks and guinea-pigs. There are lambs to be bottle-fed and cows to be milked, while a tractor ride around the farm enables the children to see how the farm works as a whole. In addition there are an African Farmyard, which supports the 'Send a Cow' charity, and an exhibition of farm life as experienced by the Legge family through the generations.

St Peter's Church, Bromyard

Right: Lower Brockhampton

Below: The Garden at Bannut

Places to Visit

Around Ledbury

Hellens
Much Marcle, HR8 2LY
☎ 01531 660504.
www.hellensmanor.com
info@hellensmanor.com
Manor House and gardens containing a wealth of period furnishings, paintings and decorations.
Open: Wed, Thu, Sun, and Bank Holiday Mon afternoons; entry is by guided tour at 2pm, 3pm and 4pm.
Location: near village of Much Marcle, just off the A449 between Ledbury and Ross-on-Wye

Westons Cider
Much Marcle, HR8 2NQ
☎ 01531 660108
www.westons-cider.co.uk
Modern cider mill, tours, farm park, cafe
Open: all year, Mon-Fri 9-4.30; Sat-Sun, Bank Hols 10-4
Location: ½ mile west of A449 near Much Marcle

16th Century Painted Room
Town Council Offices, Church Lane, Ledbury, HR8 1DH
☎ 01531 632306
One of the best examples of Elizabethan wall painting
Location: Town Centre, to rear of Market House

Butcher Row Museum
Church Lane, Ledbury, HR8 1DW
☎ 01531 632040
Small museum containing a range of artifacts on Victorian and local life
Open: daily 11-5 (Good Fri to 30 Sep); 11-3 (Oct)
Admission is free

Eastnor Castle
Ledbury, HR8 1RL
☎ 01531 633160
www.eastnorcastle.com
enquiries@eastnorcastle.com
Fairytale castle, deer park, arboretum and lake, maze, adventure playground
Cafe and gift shop
Programme of special events (contact for current details)
Open: 11-4.30 on Easter Weekend, May Bank Holiday Weekends, Sun (mid Jun-end Sep) &
Mon-Thu (mid Jul–end Aug)
Location: 2 miles east of Ledbury, off A449 and A438

Frome Valley Vineyard
Paunton Court, Bishops Frome,WR6 5BJ
☎ 01885 490768
www.fromewine.co.uk
jeanie@fromewine.co.uk
Local vineyard producing a range of white wines from dry to medium sweet
Open: Apr–Oct, Wed-Sun and Bank Holiday Mon 11.30-5
Location: 4 miles south of Bromyard off B4214

Hop Pocket Craft Centre
Bishops Frome WR6 5BT
☎ 01531 640323
www.the hoppocket.com
info@thehoppocket.com
Open: Tue-Sat 10-5.30, Sun 12-5 (not Tue in Jan–Feb)
Closed: Mon (except Bank Holidays)

Around Bromyard

The Time Machine Dr. Who Museum
Bromyard HR7 4BP
☎ 01885 488329
www.timemachineuk.com
Displays of television, film, and science fiction models and toys; cafe.
Open: Apr-Sep (daily 10.30-5), Oct-Mar (Weds-Sun, 11-4)
Location: The Square, Bromyard

The Garden at the Bannut
Bringsty WR6 5TA
☎ 01885 482206
www.bannut.co.uk
3 acres of formal and informal gardens
Tearoom and plant sales
Open: Easter–Sep (12.30-5 Wed, Sat, Sun, Bank Hols)
Location: 2½ miles east of Bromyard on A44 Worcester road

Brockhampton Estate (incl. Lower Brockhampton)
Bringsty, WR6 5TB
☎ 01885 488099/482077
www.nationaltrust.org.uk
brockhampton@nationaltrust.org.uk
Country estate and moated manor house, walks and trails, tearoom
Open: Estate and parkland – all year
House – afternoons in Mar-Oct (Wed-Sun)
Location: 2 miles east of Bromyard on the A44

Moors Meadow Garden
Bromyard, HR7 4LZ
☎ 01885 410318
www.moorsmeadow.co.uk
7 acre organic hillside garden overlooking the Kyre valley
Open: end Mar–early Sep, 11-5 (Fri-Sun and Bank Holiday Mon); other times by arrangement.
Location: 4 miles north of Bromyard off the B4214

Shortwood Family Farm
Pencombe, HR7 4RP
☎ 01885 400205
www.shortwoodfarm.co.uk
Organic working dairy farm with hands-on activities and friendly animals
Tearoom and shop
Open: Apr–early Sep and Oct half-term week (daily) ; mid Sep–mid Oct (weekends)
Location: near village of Pencombe, 5 miles SW of Bromyard

3 Leominster and the North

The north of the county contains Herefordshire's second main market town, Leominster. The area is dominated by rolling countryside full of small villages, secluded valleys, wooded hills, and ancient settlements whose history stretches back through medieval times to the Saxons, Romans and Celts. There are also some fine country houses, such as Berrington Hall and Croft Castle as well as plenty of attractive villages, with interesting houses, cottages and churches to explore. There is some excellent walking country here and, for those wanting a longer route, The Mortimer Trail winds its way over the hills and through villages and over the border into Shropshire. The Welsh hills of old Radnorshire are within easy reach, as are the towns of Presteigne, Knighton and Ludlow, which lie beyond the county border.

Opposite page: Croft Castle
Left: Shobdon Arches Tympanum

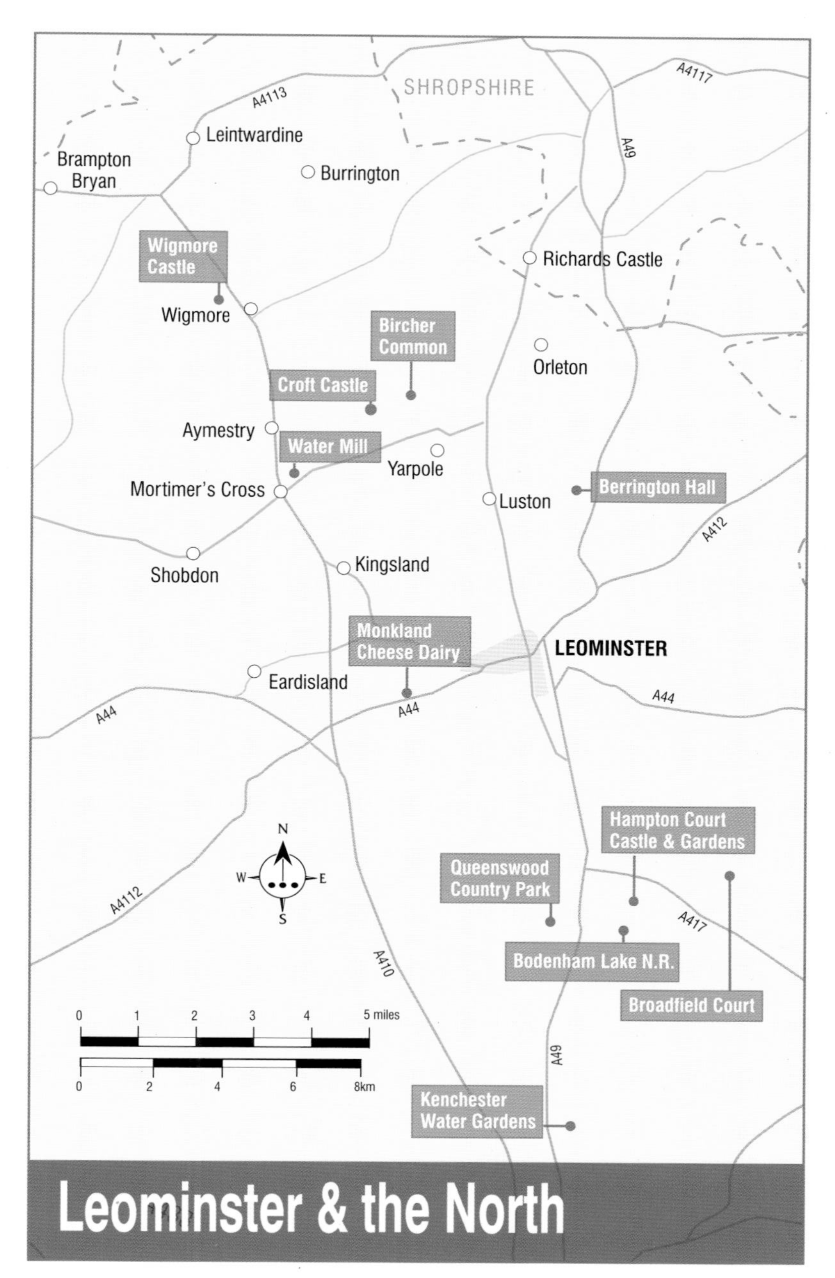

Leominster & the North

Hereford to Leominster

The A49 takes heads north out of Hereford towards Leominster. Two miles north of the city beside the busy main road at Pipe and Lyde are **Kenchester Water Gardens**. Enthusiasts of things aquatic will enjoy the 6ac/2.5ha of gardens and landscaped pools, stocked with tropical and cold water fish. If you are looking for inspiration then there is plenty on offer and it is one of the largest aquatic centres in this part of the country. It is also very much a commercial operation and you can pretty much buy anything you see as you stroll around. The church which stands just to the north is dedicated to St. Peter and was significantly restored in the nineteenth century – the name Pipe comes from the old Saxon saint, Pipa.

A little further north are the wooded slopes of Dinmore Hill and **Queenswood Country Park and Arboretum**. If you are looking for a place to stretch your legs, have a picnic, or entertain children outdoors there's plenty to explore here. The park has over 100ac/40ha of woodland, a surviving remnant of a much larger oak wood, which belonged to the kings of England in the Middle Ages. After being used as a site for timber production in the first part of the twentieth century it was given to the County Council and it is now a Site of Special Scientific Interest. In the 1950s an arboretum was established at the heart of the park and there are now over 650 species of trees and shrubs, whose blossom, foliage or berries bring colour and form to the place at any time of year. You can wander off along the extensive network of paths, or follow one of the three way-marked trails. The main paths in the Arboretum are level, with a crushed stone surface, and have been designed with accessibility in mind. There is also a children's play area, picnic facilities, a cafe and an information centre, housed in the buildings near the car park – and in fact these buildings have all been rescued from elsewhere in the county and re-erected on the site: the cafe was once a seventeenth century pub in Hereford and the Information Centre a tannery in Leominster. In addition there is a programme of countryside events which starts in May and continues through to December.

To the southeast of Dinmore Hill is another area of countryside worth visiting. **Bodenham Lake Nature Reserve** is a 110ac/45ha area of former gravel pits. There are riverside meadows, old and newly planted orchards, woodlands and the lake itself is the largest area of open water in the county. It is a tranquil place for a walk and an important winter-feeding area for wildfowl. Some of the site is closed to the public to protect the wildlife but there is still plenty to look out for, such as otters, great crested grebes, cormorants and kestrels.

To the north of Dinmore Hill, and less than a mile down the A417 Gloucester road from the junction with the A49, is **Hampton Court Castle and Gardens**. The castle dates from the fifteenth century and is set in over 1,000ac/407ha of estate and parkland. Until 2009 it was not possible to visit the castle itself, but now the state rooms have been opened to the public. However, it is the gardens that are the main draw for visitors. The River Lugg flows through the grounds and the wooded slopes of Dinmore Hill provide a dramatic background. The original Victorian garden now includes new flower beds and areas divided by canals, ornamental walkways, fountains and island pavilions. There is a maze of a thousand yew trees with a gothic tower at its centre, from which you can gain a panoramic view of the area, a wisteria tunnel takes you to the lawns beside the castle and beyond there are riverside and woodland walks. Much of the produce grown in the kitchen garden supplies the Orangery Cafe, a grand conservatory, designed by Joseph Paxton, adjoining the castle. There is also a garden shop, in the garden bothy, which sells plants from the garden, homemade produce from the castle kitchens and local crafts and gifts. In addition, there is a programme of events, such as outdoor theatre and activities in the grounds.

While in this part of the county wine buffs might take the opportunity to visit the local vineyard, a couple of miles north of Bodenham, at **Broadfield Court**. The estate has been in existence since Norman times and parts of the current house date from the fourteenth century. The current owners, the James family, moved here in the 1960s and started the Broadfield vineyard at the start of the 1970s. It is now one of the most mature vineyards in the country and the largest in Herefordshire, extending to 13ac/5ha. You can taste the varieties of wine produced here and there are also tours of the vineyard if you wish to learn more about the processes and techniques of viticulture. You can also wander around the walled kitchen garden whose centre piece is a David Austin rose garden, which boasts over thirty varieties. The garden also supplies the cafe and there is a shop where their wine is on sale.

Leominster

The town of **Leominster** (pronounced *Lemster*) is situated on the banks of the River Lugg at the crossroads of the A49 and the A44. It has long been a market town and its history goes back to pre-Norman times. It is still a busy place and is known as the county's second town. Tradition has it that the town was the home of the Ryeland sheep, famed for its soft and dense wool, known as Lemster Ore, and that this accounted for much of the town's wealth in the Middle Ages.

The centre of the town is **Corn Square**, where markets are still held, a weekly one on Fridays and a farmers' market on the second Saturday of each month. Many of the houses and shops in the centre are of timber construction, though some have been rendered in brick or stone, and this part of the town has largely escaped the blight of twentieth century concrete. **Drapers Lane** heads north from the centre and is full of small independent shops and half-timbered buildings. It also houses the Tourist Information Centre in the former printing offices of the Leominster News. Parallel with Drapers Lane is the main High Street. At the junction with Broad Street, Church Road leads down to **Leominster Priory and Church**.

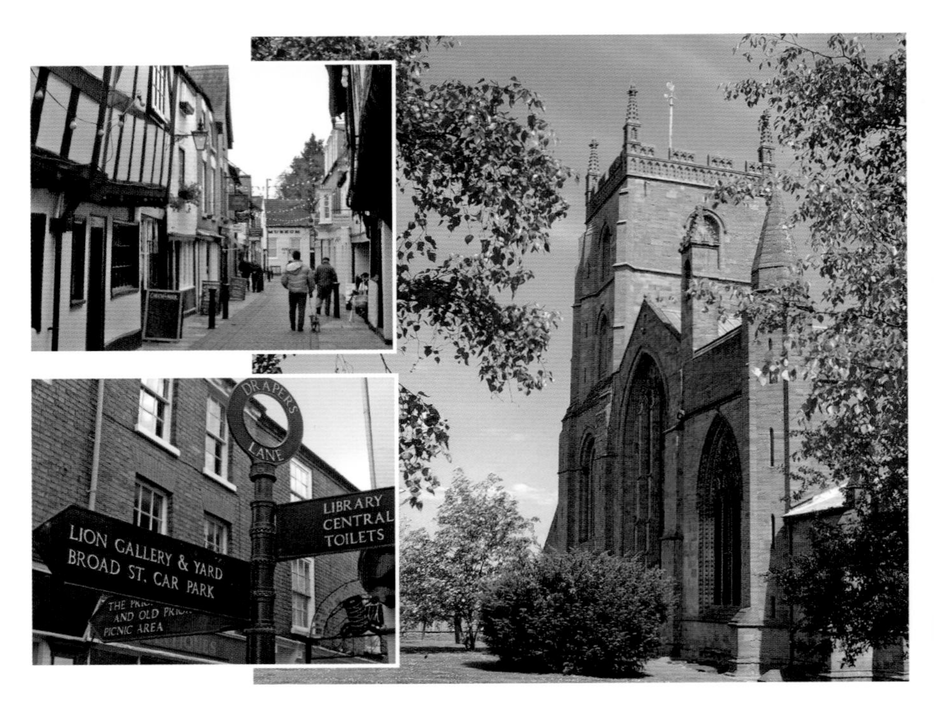

Top left: School Lane, Leominster Above left: Drapers Lane, Leominster
Above: Leominster Priory

Monkland Dairy, cheesemaking

Above: Berrington Hall

Above: Hampton Court Gardens

What strikes you immediately about the church of St. Peter and St. Paul is its massive size. From the outside it looks more like a small cathedral and the interior does nothing to disappoint these expectations. It is thought that the foundation goes back to a Saxon religious community but the oldest remains are the Norman nave of the Benedictine Abbey which was founded by monks in the twelfth century. Of the larger monastic complex only Priory House survived the ravages of Henry VIII. The two parallel naves, built in the thirteenth and fourteenth centuries, create a sense of immense space and airiness. This atmosphere has been increased further by the slender Gothic arcade which Sir Gilbert Scott designed in the nineteenth century to replace a row of Tuscan pillars. In addition you'll find a host of other architectural delights – the south aisle also has a series of fourteenth century windows; the west wall has a rare painted consecration cross; the capitals of the west door are decorated with twelfth century carvings of the Leominster School, the right hand one depicting some tiny figures of Samson and the Lion; there is a painted Wheel of Life which can be glimpsed through the windows above the wooden screen of the choir vestry; and there is a well-preserved ducking stool last used 200 years ago.

From the church it is a short walk southwards to the public park, known as The Grange. Here you'll see a timbered building on its eastern side. This is **Grange Court**, Leominster's former market hall which originally stood at the junction of the High Street and Broad Street. It was built by the King's carpenter John Abel in 1633 and the ground floor was then open. It was moved and re-erected in its current position in the middle of the nineteenth century as a private residence. It now houses council offices, though the exterior makes for interesting viewing as there are a number of inscriptions and unusual carvings.

A little further on is Etnam Street which houses the small **Leominster Folk Museum**. Here you'll find varied displays and objects, many donated by locals, which tell the story of the town from pre-Roman times to the present day. The collection comprises artefacts, pictures, photographs, postcards and documents, including paintings and drawings by famous local Victorian artist John Scarlett Davis. The museum is also carrying out a project to record peoples' reminiscences and memories, creating a living archive of oral history for the future.

If you happen to be visiting in early June you might want to catch some of the cultural events which are held as part of the **Leominster Festival**. Over almost three decades the arts festival has featured a range of music concerts, including jazz, classical, and folk, as well as talks by authors, exhibitions by artists, films, drama and poetry recitals, and the Birmingham Philharmonic Orchestra has regularly attended.

If you fancy trying locally produced cheeses and seeing how they are made then a couple of miles west of Leominster along the A44 is **Monkland Cheese Dairy**. The owners have been making cheese here in a converted barn and former cider mill for almost fifteen years. Their approach is to combine traditional recipes and techniques with a more modern approach and they have contributed to something of a cheese revival in this part of the world. Local ingredients are used where possible and the actual cheese-making takes place just through the back doors of the cafe and shop. You can join a guided tour and have the details of the processes explained by the staff, who not only make the cheese but also research the recipes they use. Tasting the varieties is part of the experience and the range of flavours comes as quite a surprise. Varieties include Little Hereford, made to a traditional local recipe, Hereford Sage, Oak-Smoked Little Hereford, and Monkland, which is bathed in brine. It is a quaint place and shows just what small-scale operators can produce. The owners also have a number of Mouse-trap Cheese Shops in Leominster, Hereford and Ludlow. The shop also sells other varieties of British cheese and local foods.

Leominster to Richards Castle

If you are looking to visit country houses in the area there are two to chose from. The first is **Berrington Hall,** three miles to the north of Leominster, signed off the A49. This impressive house was built for Thomas Harley, a wealthy banker in the eighteenth century. Henry Holland was engaged to design the neo-classical mansion, while his father-in-law, the famous landscape designer 'Capability' Brown laid out the formal gardens. The house and grounds are situated in a stunning setting overlooking the Herefordshire countryside, with views stretching to the Black Mountains. Inside the house there are collections of furniture and paintings, displays of costumes and much of the interior décor is in exquisite condition. It all enables a visitor to gain a clear idea of just how splendid the mansion was in its heyday. You can also nose around the below-stairs areas of the servants' quarters, the laundry and the dairy and stables. The gardens are a joy to wander around on a sunny day. There are a walled garden with an orchard of traditional Herefordshire apple varieties, a large ornamental lake, and waymarked trails or guided tours to the rest of the parkland. In addition, there are a children's play area and tearooms. If you want to stay the night you can even hire one of the holiday cottages on the estate.

Travelling north from Leominster on the B4361 you soon pass through the village of **Luston**. It still has a pub, the unusually named Balance Inn and, a few doors down, a striking black and white Tudor house called The Knapp. **Yarpole** lies a little to the west and is worth visiting if only because it is an exceptionally pretty village. The unusual name means fish pool, and there is still a Fishpool Valley to the northwest. In fact there are several good reasons to detour. The church of Saint Leonard has one of Herefordshire's seven detached bell towers. This one has had its timbers dated to the end of the twelfth century, making it one of the oldest surviving timber structures in the country. It stands to the south of its church, with a weather-boarded upper storey giving it a homely look.

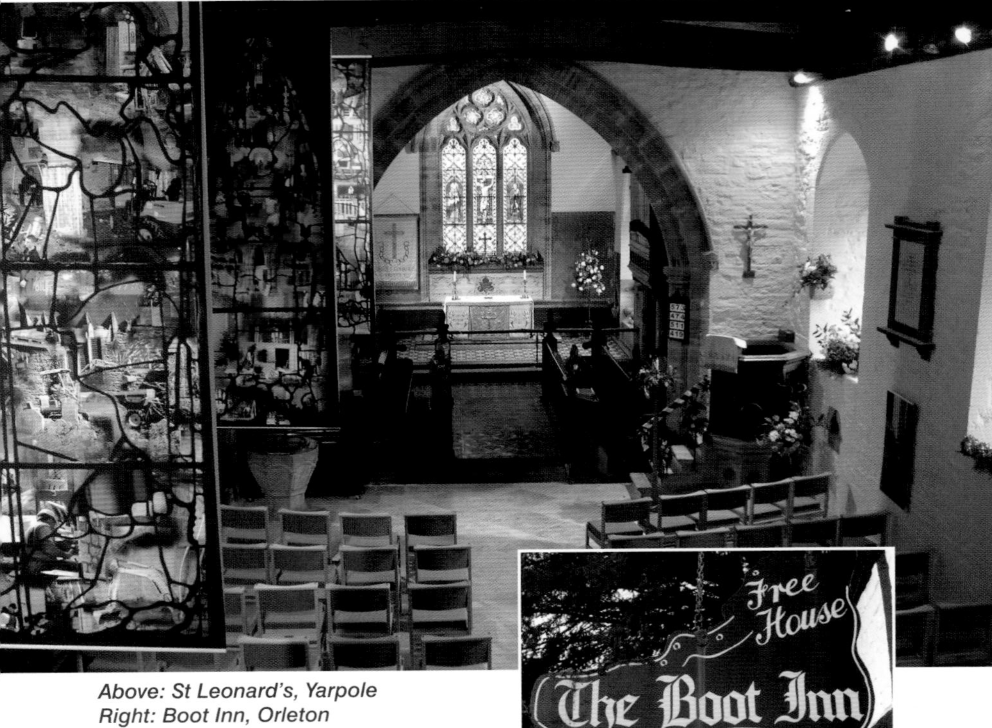

Above: St Leonard's, Yarpole
Right: Boot Inn, Orleton

However, there is a more modern but no less impressive development inside the church. Here, recent fundraising for a community project has enabled a significant amount of renovation and the building now houses the village Post Office and stores. A little way up from the church, there is also a pub, the Bell Inn.

To the north is **Bircher Common**, which, now managed by the National Trust, covers an area of almost 350ac/141ha, making it one of the largest commons in Herefordshire. It is still subject to commoners' and graziers' rights and is a haven for wildlife in the area, with colonies of butterflies and a varied bird community. Here, there is year round unrestricted walking over the slopes of the common, through woodlands of birch, oak and conifers, and in the steep-sided valleys. Adjacent is the **Croft Estate and Croft Castle**, also now under the management of the National Trust. The estate has belonged to the Croft family for thirty generations and contains the ancient Croft Ambrey hill fort, whose occupation dates back to the fourth century BC and whose slopes are studded with old beech, oak and chestnut trees. The Fishpool Valley is particularly dramatic and in the late eighteenth century it was landscaped to include ornamental structures such as a grotto and pump house, having in medieval times contained a series of fish pools. Croft Castle itself is a seventeenth century castellated manor house, though there was an actual castle, or series of castles, built on the site from Norman times, whose earthwork remains can be seen in the meadow nearby. Inside the house you are confronted with period furniture, paintings and interiors in the Gothic style. Outside there are a walled garden with an orchard, tearooms and a children's play area. In addition, there are three waymarked trails around the parkland and the estate. Here too, as at Berrington Hall, you can have an extended stay in one of the two estate cottages.

North of Yarpole is **Orleton**, lying to the east of the B4361. This is another small village with some fine black and white timbered houses, including The Boot Inn, which was originally three shops, a butchers, a funeral parlour, and a cobblers, hence the name, though this might stem from the old practice of serving beer and cider in a 'jack' or 'boot'. Whatever the true origin, it is an atmospheric and picturesque place for a drink. At the other end of the village lies St. George's church, worth seeing for its timber spire and twelfth century font with Romanesque carvings.

Richards Castle stands just short of the county boundary with Shropshire. A left turn by The Castle pub up the hill past black and white timbered Court House for a mile brings you to the site of the church and castle. There is a small parking area near Old Church Cottage and a short walk beyond brings you up to one of the reasons why the church of St. Bartholomew is well known, its detached bell tower. The church was abandoned at the end of the nineteenth century but has nevertheless been well-preserved and it is worth having a look inside for its seventeenth century box pews. For those wanting a detailed tour, the Churches Conservation Trust have produced an excellent explanatory leaflet, available at the rear of the church. There is also an informative Millennium Map on the southern edge of the churchyard, with interesting snippets about the area's history and associations. The remains of the castle, one of the oldest in Wales and already in ruins by the sixteenth century, lies just a little further on beyond the graveyard.

St Bartholomew's Tower and Box Pews, Richards Castle

Leominster to Leintwardine

To the northwest of Leominster the first sizeable village is **Kingsland**. Strung out along the B4360, many of the houses date from the sixteenth or seventeenth centuries and have characteristic blackened timbers.A number of the buildings have been fronted with brick, added from the eighteenth century onwards. The best examples of these are in the centre of the village near the Angel Inn. Here, there is also the village post office and stores, which has a tearoom hidden in its back room. Opposite is the church of St. Michael and All Angels. What is striking about this church is its sheer size, in particular the massive west tower, which has gargoyles on its parapet. Inside, off the north porch, is a Volka chapel, which is thought to have been built as a chantry chapel for the uttering of prayers for those killed in the Battle of Mortimer's Cross in 1461. The actual site of this battle lies in Great West Field, beyond the northwestern end of the village, where there is a roadside memorial to this decisive event in the Wars of the Roses, when Edward Mortimer defeated the Lancastrians before going on to London to be crowned Edward IV. To the west of the church, along a footpath, lies the mound of a Norman castle.

A mile and a half along the A4110, at the junction with the B4362, is the settlement of **Mortimer's Cross**. Opposite the Mortimer's Cross Inn is an eighteenth century water mill, whose workings are on display, though opening times are restricted. There are also small exhibitions about the Battle of Mortimer's Cross and about micro hydro-electricity and alternative energy.

A couple of miles west, along the B4362, is the village of **Shobdon**, famous for its folly of Romanesque Arches and the Gothick interior of its church. These lie half a mile to the north of the village and can be accessed either on foot along a path up from the black and yellow Bateman Arms pub or, by car, up the lane just east of the village. Although now curiously right next to some factory sheds, it still makes for a stunning setting. A tree-lined avenue leads up from the parking area to the Arches. These are the remains of Norman church and they were moved here in the eighteenth century to form a picturesque viewpoint. Now faded but still visible you can see the twelfth century carvings on the semi-circular tympana and the supporting pillars. The interior of the church, with its extravagant decoration in the style known as Strawberry Hill Gothick, comes as a complete surprise, one that is liked or loathed. There is a guide book for those wanting detailed explanations of the architecture and history of both structures.

Aymestrey contains a church built of local limestone, with a fine carved rood screen, an unusual bier with pneumatic tyres, and is dedicated to John the Baptist and the little known St. Alkmund, an Anglo-Saxon saint of the eighth century. Behind the church is the attractive Aymestry Court, worth a look from the end of the graveyard for its weathered timbers and yellow pannelling. At the far end of the village, beyond its sprinkling of old houses, lies the Riverside Inn, where the western branch of the former Roman road of Watling Street crosses the Lugg.

Almost all visitors to **Wigmore** head for one of the two pubs and the castle, which stands on a hill above the town. There is no direct vehicular access and cars are directed to a car park in the village near the school. However, it makes for a pleasant walk up past the medieval St. James' Church, which itself is worth visiting for the herringbone masonry in the north wall of the nave, the linenfold pannelling on the sixteenth century pulpit, and the unusual arrangement of pews in the chancel. The castle itself lies a few hundred metres further up the hill, along a footpath. It is now under the management of English Heritage who have recently made considerable efforts to preserve what remains of the gatehouse, the walls and the towers. By design it has been left in a somewhat wild condition and this is all to the good for those who like to think of castles as places of bygone romance and intrigue. The place was home to the powerful Mortimer family, the so-called Lords of the Marches, who added significantly to the buildings during the twelfth to the fifteenth centuries. However, it was deliberately destroyed in the seventeenth century during the period of the Civil War to prevent its being used as a base by Royalists. For those wanting more in the way of history, rather than romance, dotted around the site are the expected English Heritage information boards.

To the north, devotees of ecclesiastical artefacts may wish to detour right, off the A4110 and past the former Wigmore Abbey, whose ruins can be viewed from the road, towards the isolated settlement of **Burrington** and its church of St. George. Most who make the trek here do so to see the timber spire and the series of cast iron grave slabs, which lie outside at the foot of the east wall. They are notable also for their simple and plain lettering.

Situated in the Teme Valley to the southwest of Leintwardine is an area of farmland and low-lying but steepsided hills stretching towards the border with Wales. The pretty village of **Brampton Bryan** is worth a detour, if only to see its range of old houses and cottages and its magnificent yew hedge. The church of St. Barnabas has a fine hammerbeam roof, an unusually wide nave, and a somewhat grim history. It was built in the 1650s during the time of the Commonwealth after the previous structure, the castle, and indeed much of the village was destroyed in a siege during the Civil War. Now however it is a tranquil place, with a good teashop and excellent walking on the Brampton Bryan estate, a former deer park. For book fiends, there is the added bonus of Aardvark Books, housed in a barn behind the main street, with a stock of over 50,000 titles.

The village of **Leintwardine** is reached across a medieval stone bridge, just downstream from the confluence of the Teme and the Clun. Close to the borders with Shropshire and Wales and surrounded by fortified hills, there is a real sense of place and history here. The old road, which runs parallel to the main A4113 up through the village, is still called Watling Street. Indeed it has long been known that the current village lies on top of the Roman site

Above: Cottages, Brampton Bryan

Left: Mortimers Cross Watermill

of Bravonium, as recorded in the Antonine Itinerary, a second century AD Roman road atlas. The OS map for the area prints the alternative name, Branogenium, and this is the name assigned to the place by the geographer Ptolemy. Whichever name was actually used you can still see hard evidence of Roman occupation in the Norman doorway of the west wall of the Church of St. Mary Magdalene. Here there are tell-tale thin Roman bricks, reclaimed from some building or ruin and placed either side of the window. Of interest inside the church are carvings on the roof timbers and pillars in the nave, some decorative stone screens flanking the east window, a disused sixteenth century clock, and in the vestry a memorial to Sir Banastre Tarleton. To some he has come to be known as 'Bloody Ban', following his reputation for military ruthlessness in the American War of Independence, though some recent books and films have treated him in a more heroic light. Back down towards the bottom end of the village, there are two pubs, The Lion, on the main road, and The Sun, which is still in use as a parlour pub, on Rosemary Lane. In addition, there is a Community Centre, which includes a small display of Roman artefacts.

Black and White Villages

Herefordshire is well known for its plethora of villages and towns dominated by black and white timbered houses and barns. Many of these buildings date from the sixteenth and seventeenth centuries, with some built even earlier. At times they provide merely a picturesque backdrop, while some buildings are historically significant and are perhaps the last surviving examples of their type in the country.

Many black and white timbered structures are clustered in the north and northwest of the county but this style of building can be seen throughout Herefordshire. An official Black and White Village Trail has been created between the towns of Leominster and Kington and passes through some of the prettiest countryside the county has to offer. The 40 mile trail, designed initially as a car route, begins at Leominster and from here leads to Weobley, Eardisley, Kington, Pembridge, Eardisland, and then back to Leominster. Since its inception the trail has inspired a cycling and walking route, and even an accommodation route for those wanting to stay and sleep among the blackened timbers. Details and trail booklets are available form tourist information centres throughout the county.

The construction of many of the earlier timbered buildings is based on the cruck frame. Medieval builders perfected the art of finding naturally curving timber, or training trees for this purpose. A cruck frame consists of a pair of curved timbers, called blades, which were often cut from one tree to form a curving 'A' frame. This way of building a house's frame had the advantage that the weight of the roof was taken directly through the blades to the ground, while the walls were merely braced to the frame itself. The cruck frames themselves had to be assembled on the ground, being shaped by an adze, then tenoned and morticed, before being holed and pinned together with wooden pegs. Once hoisted into position they were joined to a ridge timber running the length of the building, in this way forming an open hall below. It was only at this stage that the walls were added. Their main purpose was to keep out the weather rather than to bear weight, so anything weatherproof could be used, clay, wattle and daub, and later stone. An alternative, and somewhat later, method of construction is the box frame. Made of vertical and horizontal timbers, its main advantage was that it allowed the building of second and third floors. This was essential when building in town centres as it made greater use of the available space, and it also meant wings could be added still further increasing the capacity.

Today many of these buildings have the contrasting appearance of blackened timbers and white-washed wall panels, so characteristic of villages in Herefordshire, and indeed elsewhere in England. Originally many buildings would have been left unblackened for the timbers to weather naturally, but it gradually became the custom from Elizabethan times to blacken the timbers by tarring them with weather-proofing pitch, with this style and colour scheme becoming more popular in its own right in the nineteenth century.

Places to Visit

Hereford to Leominster

Kenchester Water Gardens
Lyde, HR1 3AB
☎ 01432 270981
www.kenchesterwatergardens.co.uk
aquatic centre with gardens and tearooms
Open: all year (daily)
Location: on A49, 2 miles north of Hereford

Queenswood Country Park
Dinmore Hill, HR6 0PY
☎ 01432 260848
www.herefordshire.gov.uk/queenswood
100 acre park and woodlands, cafe, information centre
Open: park (all year), Information Centre (Mar-Dec, daily, 10-4.30)
Location: on the A49 at top of Dinmore hill between Hereford and Leominster

Hampton Court Castle and Gardens
Hope Under Dinmore, HR6 0PN
☎ 01568 797777
www.hamptoncourt.org.uk
office@hamptoncourt.org.uk
Historic house, gardens and parkland, tearooms.
Open: Gardens: Apr-Oct 11-5 daily (not Mon, except Bank Hols); Castle tours: Tue-Thurs
Location: off the A417, near the junction with A49 between Hereford and Leominster.

Broadfield Court
Bodenham, HR1 3LG
☎ 01568 797918
www.broadfieldcourt.co.uk
info@broadfieldcourt.co.uk
Old English gardens, vineyard, cafe, wine tasting
Open: all year (daily 10-4)
Location: off A417, 2 miles from the junction with A49 between Hereford and Leominster.

Leominster

Leominster Folk Museum
Etnam Street, HR6 8AL
☎ 01568 615186
www.leominstermuseum.org.uk
Collections of artefacts illustrating local life
Open: Easter-Oct, incl Bank Hols (Mon-Fri 11-4, Sat 10.30-1.30)
Admission is free
Location: town centre, on Etnam Street opposite entrance to School Lane (which leads to Corn Square)

Monkland Cheese Dairy
Monkland HR6 9DB
☎ 01568 720307
www.mousetrapcheese.co.uk
Cheesemaking cafe and farm shop
Cheesemaking viewing Mon, Wed, Fri 10-2
Open: all year 10-5
Location: 2 miles west of Leominster on A44

Leominster to Richards Castle

Berrington Hall
Leominster HR6 0DW
☎ 01568 615721
www.nationaltrust.org.uk
berrington@nationaltrust.org.uk
Neo-classical house and gardens, parkland, tearoom.
Open: House: Mar-Nov (Mon-Weds, Sat-Sun 1-5); Garden & Grounds: Feb-Dec (days and times vary)
Location: 3 miles north of Leominster on west side of A49

Croft Castle
Yarpole HR6 9PW
☎ 01568 780246
www.nationaltrust.org.uk
croftcastle@nationaltrust.org.uk
17th century castellated mansion, gardens, parkland, walks, tearoom
Open: Parkland: all year; Castle: Mar-Oct 1-5 (Wed-Sun, & Mon-Tue in Aug), Nov-Dec 1-4 (Sat-Sun); Garden: as castle but 11-5
Location: 5 miles NW of Leominster off B4362

Leominster to Leintwardine

Mortimer's Cross Water Mill
Lucton HR6 9PE
☎ 01568 708820
www.mortimerscrossmill.com
18th century water mill, local history and hydro-electricity displays
Open: Apr-Sep, Sun only, 10-4
Location: between Hereford and Leintwardine on B4362 near junction with A4110

Aardvark Books
Brampton Bryan SY7 0DH
☎ 01547 530888
www.aardvark-books.com
Book barn, new and secondhand books, cafe
Open: Mon-Fri 9-5, Sat 10-5, & Sun 10-4 (Jul-Aug, Dec only)
Location: just off A4113 at Brampton Bryan

4. Kington and the West

The far west of the county has long been true border country. The land around the market town of Kington looks as much east into England as it does the opposite direction into Wales. Although there are a number of villages, such as Pembridge, Weobley and Eardisley, which are peppered with the black and white timbered buildings reminiscent of places further east in the county, the lie of the land starts to change and become more recognizable as hill country. Cutting through the middle of this western section is the broadening Wye Valley, where the river meanders towards Hereford. To the south lies the border town of Hay-on-Wye, now famous for its literary associations, and the uplands of the Black Mountains. These are true hills, whose northern ridges lie in the county and provide stunning views on clear days, and, hidden in the folds of the land to the north of these hills, is the secluded Golden Valley.

Opposite page: River Wye at Bredwardine

Left: Hay-on-Wye

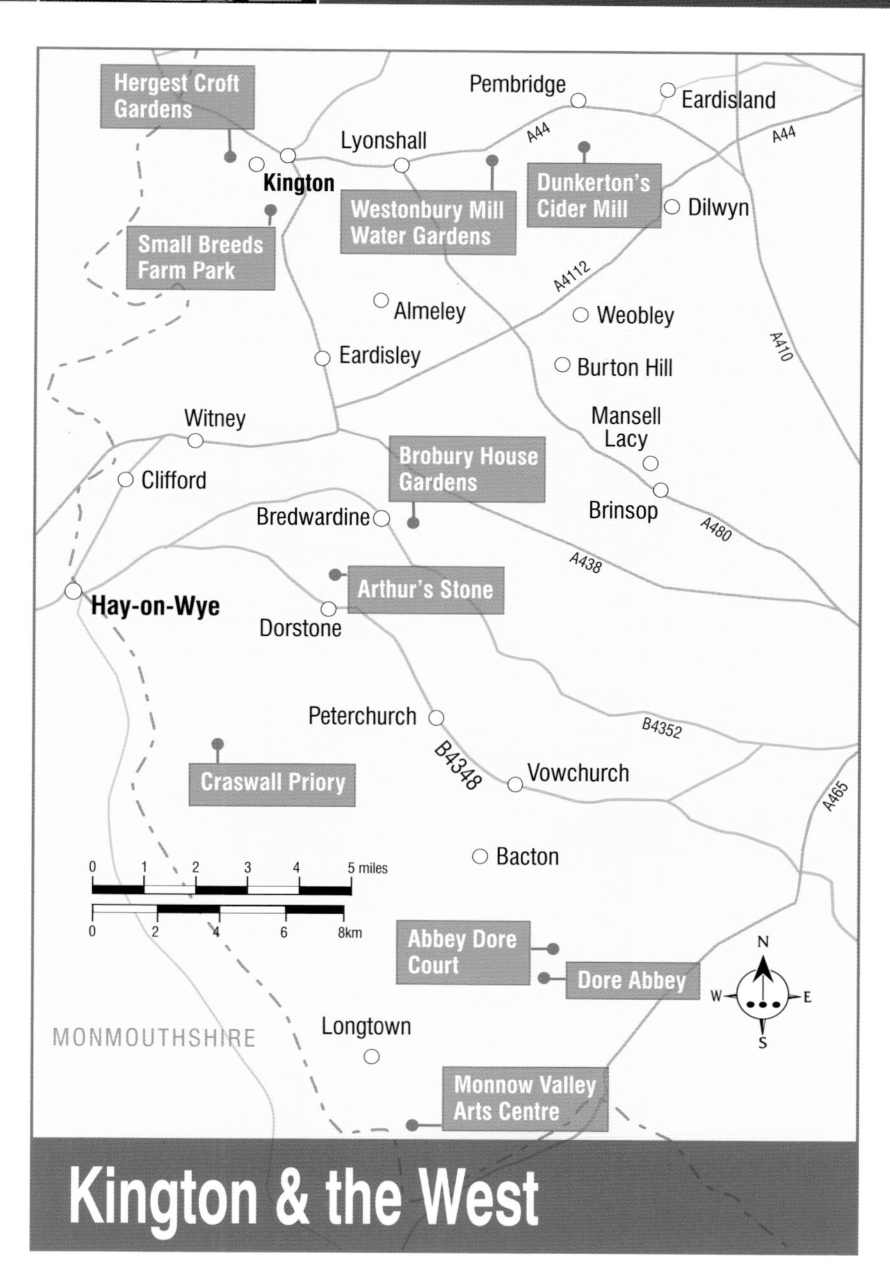

Kington & the West

Kington

The market town of **Kington** is situated in the Arrow Valley in the far west of the county, twenty miles or so from Hereford. Enclosed to the north by the hills of the Radnor Forest and to the west by the high ground of Bradnor Hill and Hergest Ridge, the town has long been part of England even though it lies to the west of Offa's Dyke, with the modern Welsh Border only a couple of miles away. Legend has it that the name Kington, or King's Town, commemorates the confiscation of lands by Harold Godwinson (later of Battle of Hastings fame) who made a gift of the area to King Edward the Confessor after a Welsh attack on Hereford in 1055, in which the city was sacked by the forces of Llewellyn of Powys. However, there are other theories that the even older, original name was Keynton, from Keya or Kine, signifying a place for selling cattle, or that the Saxon name was Chingtune. Thus, perhaps either required only a slight linguistic adaptation in the eleventh century to redesignate the town's allegiance and status.

The town itself grew up between the River Arrow, which flows to the south of the town, and the Bach Brook to the north, and lies on the old drovers' route from Wales to the English markets of Herefordshire. Indeed, Kington's cattle market used to take place on Bridge Street, and the former commons on Bradnor Hill and Hergest Ridge made the town a favoured stopping point. Now the main A44 loops around to the east and north, by-passing the centre. Yet Kington can still be a bustling place and even now has the air of a town that exists for its local residents as well as the tourist trade.

The middle of the town is dominated by the red-brick Victorian Market Hall, with its clock tower commemorating Queen Victoria's golden jubilee in 1887. Nearby, along Mill Street, local history is on display at **Kington Museum**, where admission is free. It houses an eclectic mix of items, mostly received from residents of the town or the surrounding area in an attempt to show the history of the town through local eyes. The main collections cover textiles and clothes from Victorian times onwards, domestic items, tools and implements and ephemera from local industries and craftmaking, and militaria from the world wars of the twentieth century. For real local history enthusiasts the museum holds an extensive collection of photographs of the town and its inhabitants.

The town's High Street still contains a good number of independent, local shops, something of a rarity these days even for a market town as historic and in some senses isolated as Kington, and plenty of pubs or cafes to choose from. You still get the sense that the shops here have a purpose beyond a mere cash nexus – they actually stock things you might need, whether as a local resident shopping for essentials, a tourist in search of lunch, or perhaps a walker in need of a plaster for blisters.

If you have the energy and inclination a walk up the hill along Church Street leads predictably up past the Swan Hotel, with its delightful square set back from the road, to the **church of Saint Mary**. Set in a commanding position overlooking the town, its eighteenth century spire, built on a twelfth century tower, is a landmark for miles around. Inside there is a great feeling of space, a Norman font with rope moulding, some exquisite lancet windows in the chancel depicting the twelve apostles in Victorian stained glass, and in the south aisle the fifteenth century effigies and tomb of Thomas Vaughan, of nearby Hergest Court, and his wife Ellen Gethin. He was known as the Black Vaughan, and she as Ellen the Terrible. Quite what Thomas did to earn this name is lost to history – he was killed in the Wars of the Roses but returned to haunt the inhabitants of Kington until twelve parsons with twelve candles enticed his restless spirit into a snuff box which they duly hurled into nearby Hergest Pool. Ellen's posthumous reputation has fared better, though still grim enough. She had dressed as a man in order to enter an archery competition where she was able to take vengeance on a fellow competitor and murderer of her brother. They now rest side by side, the hands of each clasped together in prayer, or perhaps for forgiveness.

The town now markets itself as a centre for walking and there is certainly plenty on offer. For energetic or extended outings the long distance trail of Offa's Dyke Path leads off over Hergest Ridge and Bradnor Hill, the Mortimer Trail will take you north for thirty miles to Ludlow, while Vaughan's Way heads south to Bredwardine to join up with the Wye Valley Walk. However, if a gentler stroll is required the Herefordshire Trail provides some riverside walking along the River Arrow and Kington Tourist Information Centre, located on Mill Street opposite the museum, stocks many walking leaflets and books for walks in the area and around the town, its historical buildings, back lanes and the burgage walls.

Kington is also good for cycling and mountain biking – in early June the town hosts the Roughride Event, one of the largest mountain bike events in Wales. Cyclists, looking for less strenuous cycling, can enjoy a network of small lanes with little traffic through unspoilt countryside to small villages and hamlets. Suggested routes can be found in the T.I.C.

If you happen to be visiting in June you'll find events and festivities organised as part of the locally run Kington Festival, while in September there is the annual Kington Show, possibly the last remaining one-day livestock show in Herefordshire. The show is a traditional agricultural show with horse, cattle, sheep, dog and horticultural classes together with shearing competitions and farrier demonstrations. A free shuttle bus runs throughout the day between the town and the showground.

To the west of the town up the hill along Ridgebourne Road lies **Hergest Croft Gardens**. Being described as a unique garden for all seasons and as having one of the finest collections of trees and shrubs in Britain is a challenge to live up to, but these gardens really can exceed even the highest expectations. For more than 100 years four generations of the Banks family have transformed what was originally open fields into four distinct gardens. Established, as many Victorian and Edwardian gardens were, along principles influenced by ideas from Japan and China, the trees and plantings have matured and developed over the more than 70ac/28ha. The Azalea garden is made even more impressive by an avenue of blue cedars; the Maple Grove contains many specimens introduced from the Far East; the Kitchen Garden is everything it should be and more besides; in addition there is the Park and Park Wood. Here, you can take a longer walk among specimen trees and down into a valley of ancient oak woodland and giant rhododendron. The effect of all this makes it a wonder that the views are to the Black Mountains of England and Wales rather than to the foothills of the Himalayas. There is also the Croquet Lawn in front of the house, where lunch and teas are served, a large rockery and a slate garden. The gardeners are happy to share their considerable horticultural knowledge, either when asked by individuals or to organised groups. Families are actively encouraged and it's a nice touch that under 16s are admitted free. Events are held throughout the year, including a Flower Fair on the first Bank Holiday in May and an Autumn Plant Fair on the second Sunday of October.

Towards Pembridge

The main A44 road eastwards from Kington soon brings you to **Lyonshall**. The church and site of an eleventh century castle stand to the north of the main road and it was around these buildings that the medieval village stood. The modern village lies off the main road to the south. It's a good place to stop off, being on the Black and White Village Trail, and it still has one pub, the Royal George, though a far cry from the seven it boasted in the nineteenth century. If you have a little more time it is worth taking a walk along the footpaths to the west of the village, along which there is a prominent section of Offa's Dyke still visible.

Continuing towards Pembridge for another two miles, there is a turning off to **Westonbury Mill Water Gardens**. These gardens have been designed by hydrologist Richard Pim around an old water mill house which dates from the 1760s. It was worked as a cornmill for about 100 years but was redundant by the start of the nineteenth century. He found the house derelict in the 1960s, restored it, and started work to convert the surrounding 3ac/1.2ha into a most unusual garden, opening to the public in 2002. Guided by the principle that a garden should not only be beautiful but also fun there is a water-spouting tower, a Bottle Dome and African Summerhouse. The Curl Brook supplies the water, which is channelled along a series of ingenious leats and sluices to produce a tangle of streams and ponds with an impressive collection of moisture-loving plants. Various bridges connect the parts of the garden and it is a delight to wander around and see what surprise lurks around the next corner. Projects for the future include the development of a wildflower meadow. There is also a tearoom in a converted barn beside the brook.

The village of **Pembridge** rightly draws a large volume of visitors – there is now a new car park and toilets signed off the main road a short walk from the centre of the village. Owing to

Hergest Croft House and Garden

Pembridge, Market Hall and New Inn

its number of timbered houses Pembridge is very much part of the Black and White Village Trail. Yet the place is not just a tourist honey-pot. Cars and lorries still use the A44 road running through the village as a main east-west route, as vehicles have done since the road first saw considerable volumes of wheeled traffic as the main London to Aberystwyth coaching route. And the traffic still has to squeeze through the point where the road narrows by the **New Inn**, which stands at the heart of the village.

In the small square behind the inn stands one of the main draws for visitors, the **Market Hall**. It is not so much a hall as a covered meeting area, but at any rate the structure underwent dendro-dating analysis in 2002 and was estimated to have been built in the first third of the fourteenth century, making it possibly the oldest market hall still to be in regular use in the country. In the posts are notches where planks for traders used to be placed on which goods would have been displayed and, at the foot of one of the posts, there is also what is thought to be one of the original mark stones, from which the word 'market' stems. In addition the earthen floor is unusual in its survival.

From the square, steps between houses lead up to the **Church of St. Mary the Virgin**. The detached bell tower comes as a something of a surprise. Its octagonal lower staging and wooden boarding are more reminiscent of Scandinavian stave churches, and, standing as it does surrounded by a well-kept lawn, the sense of space is in complete contrast to the village itself. The church itself dates back to the fourteenth century and replaced an earlier Norman building, whose only remains are two arches in the chancel. There is a thirteenth century font, some intricate carving by Herefordshire craftsmen on the reading desk and altar rails, remnants of medieval stained glass at the west end of the north aisle, and on the chancel floor there are a number of old memorial tablets. For those wanting to explore the building thoroughly there is a comprehensive guide available.

To the south of the church stands **Court House Farm**. The site was the seat of the de Pembridge family in the eleventh and twelfth centuries, before passing into the possession of the Mortimers in the fourteenth century. This is likely to have coincided with the building of the current church, with the castle being transformed into a fortified manor house. Recent excavation has brought to light various finds indicating occupation of this site stretches back even earlier to Saxon and Roman times. From the edge of the churchyard, where there is a useful information board giving details of the excavation, the moat and mound of the old castle can be seen.

The rest of the village is well worth wandering around. The Old Steppes houses a newsagents, while opposite is Sally's Pantry and bakery. Look out also at the top of Bridge Street for Duppa's Almshouses, named after a seventeenth century Bishop of Winchester and further down East Street is the **Old Chapel Gallery**, which is a good place to browse for contemporary art and craft as well as works by both established local and nationally-known artists. Further along still is the overhanging upper storey of the King's House Hostelry, notable also for its close-set vertical framing.

If you have the time to stroll to the western end of the village, West End Farm is well worth seeing as the most complete example in Pembridge of a large cruck-framed medieval open-hall house. At the bottom end of Bridge Street is the River Arrow and some pleasant walking over meadows, though the area is prone to flooding.

A couple of miles beyond Pembridge, and to the north of the A44, is the riverside village of **Eardisland**. Easily missed en route to Leominster, as the A44 now by-passes the village, it would be a shame to ignore it. There are still two inns, the Cross and the White Swan, though the village shop and school have gone. But the community has recently overseen the restoration of the **Georgian Dovecote** which stands near the bridge and serves as an information and exhibition centre for the village. There are a good number of timber-framed buildings – Staick House across the bridge dates from the fourteenth century, Bridge Cottage used to be the grammar school, and the Old Manor House has an incongruous Queen Anne frontage. The **Church of St. Mary** stands back from the main street and is notable for its eight bells and there is a new glass Millennium Screen enabling the bell-ringers to be viewed when ringing. In addition, for much of the year there is a photographic exhibition of local scenes, accompanied by prose and poetry.

Pembridge to Hereford

Clustered in a roughly triangular area of the county lying to the south of Pembridge and north-west of Hereford is an undulating region of farmland and villages. Bordered to the east by the A4110 and to the west by the A480, it is well worth exploring, especially by bike as there is a wealth of small roads and lanes which connect the villages and hamlets; and apart from on the main roads you will encounter very little traffic.

Cider drinkers will be attracted to **Dunkerton's Cider Mill**, which lies a mile up the hill to the south of Pembridge. The family makes its own cider, and perry, on site and you can see the process in action in the barns here. There is a guided leaflet if you want to know the details of how they produce their cider and visitors are welcome to taste the varieties from the barrels stored in the shop. All the cider is organic, mostly still blends from single varieties of varying sweetness, though they have recently started to produce some which are lightly carbonated. There are walks through the apple and pear orchards and you can even take your own container to fill from the barrels. In addition to cider, the family has more recently branched out into making their own chocolate, which can be sampled from the patisserie.

Just the other side of the A4112 lies the village of **Dilwyn**. Practically every house here seems to have been built in black and white timbers, whether old or modern. The village green still stands at the heart of the place, with a pub,

Above: Pembridge

Left: Apple orchard Dunkerton's Cider Mill

The Crown, on one side. The church is dedicated to St. Mary and stands on slightly elevated ground, which gives it a rather majestic feel – the oldest part is its tower of the thirteenth century, though this is topped by a much later wooden spire. It still has six bells and if you happen to be there when the bellringers are at work you might pause for thought, as one of them is inscribed, somewhat grimly, with the words "I to the church the living call, and to the grave do summons all."

A little further down the A4112 is the main settlement in this area, the village of **Weobley**. Actually, it is something more than a village but thankfully rather less than a modern town, though it is undoubtedly on every map showing the black and white villages of Herefordshire as it is one of the best surviving examples of a Tudor town in the county.

For parking head for Bell Square, just off the B4230 at the northwestern end of the village, where there is an information board and opposite you'll see the Manor House, one of the oldest buildings in Weobley. The centre is dominated by Broad Street, which used to be narrower but the houses that occupied the middle strip burned down and have been replaced by a pleasant garden. There are tearooms, pubs, and a good number of local shops, including a well-stocked bookshop, where you can find out more about the history of the village.

At the lower, northern, end of Broad Street, lies the Old Corner House, a hall house dating from the fourteenth century, the Red Lion pub, whose eastern wing is of the same era, with an even older cottage of cruck construction to the rear, and beyond you can see the impressive spire of the **Church**

of Saints Peter and Paul. Famous for being the second tallest spire in Herefordshire, it is just as noteworthy for its pinnacles which are connected to the tower by flying buttresses, with an appearance similar, if of smaller scale, to Hereford Cathedral itself. Above the Norman south doorway there is a fine sundial, with a spreading magnolia tree to the left, and there is also a churchyard cross dating from the twelfth century, which is thought itself to have replaced a Saxon one. Inside, the south aisle has some curiously carved corbel stones, the Chancel's east window unusually depicts Jesus carrying his cross, the south Transept has a finely carved piscina, and by the pulpit is a stone coffin lid with a foliated cross and an unusual cryptic pun – a mitre, not to record the occupant's episcopal status but rather the name, Bissop. Look out also for the tomb of Colonel John Birch, a notable Parliamentarian commander in the English Civil War, who in 1645 was responsible for masterminding the taking of Hereford from the Royalists. He later became governor of the city and member of Parliament for Leominster.

Weobley Village

At the top end of the village you'll find the impressively timbered Salutation Inn along Market Pitch, and a little along the High Street, the Unicorn Inn, dating from the seventeenth century. Beyond, a short walk away from the houses is the site of **Weobley Castle.** It still has some substantial earthworks and makes a good place for a picnic or for a short stroll, which can easily be extended southwards to Burton Hill. There is also a **Museum** on the aptly named Back Lane where local artefacts are on display as well as information and archives on local history.

On the south side of Burton Hill and just off the A480 is the charming village of **Mansell Lacy**. The splendidly named Yazor brook flows through the village and you could do nothing better than to wander around for half an hour. The Church of St. Michael is showing how churches can reinvent their usable space in the twenty-first century with its innovative community space and is surrounded by houses which used to be peopled by local workers such as blacksmiths, wheelwrights and agricultural labourers. Now of course this is no longer the case, but you can still get a feel what life must have been like when it was a working village.

Of historical interest are two nearby houses, both connected to leading exponents of the Picturesque Movement in the eighteenth and nineteenth centuries. Sir Uvedale Price inherited his family estate at Foxley, a little to the northwest though now a ruin, and developed his philosophical ideas on landscape with his neighbour Richard Payne Knight, who was born at Wormsley Grange, which lies to the north of the village. However, as can happen to neighbours, the two men fell out over exactly what should qualify as picturesque.

Just over one mile closer to Hereford is the small but delectable parish of **Brinsop**. At first there seems little to draw visitors off the A480 and northwards along a rather bumpy road. After all, there are only a few houses and a church, albeit set in some stunning scenery of fields surrounded by wooded hills. However, the place has an association with William Wordsworth – his wife's brother owned Brinsop Court and the Wordsworths stayed here several times. Indeed, the church commemorates this – the stained glass windows in the north wall of the Lady Chapel and the Chancel's south wall are a memorial to Wordsworth and his family. The latter is by the celebrated church architect Sir Ninian Comper, and there are other examples of his work in the church, including the nave window in the south wall nearest the chancel, the chancel screen, and the west window. In addition there is the association with St. George. The legend that it was here that George killed his dragon is depicted in the carved tympanum above the north doorway in the north aisle, along with other figures of the Herefordshire School of Carving. The exact spot of George's slaying of the dragon is reputedly in the field to the south, marked by a stone over the Dragon's Well.

To the east of Brinsop is the steep-sided **Credenhill Park Wood**. From a car park on its southeastern corner you can explore this former Iron Age hill fort on a network of woodland paths and tracks. Higher up the defensive earthworks of the hill fort are clearly visible, though now hidden in a dense covering of trees. However, the Woodland Trust now manage the site and are in the process of restoring the woodland to native broadleaved trees.

Towards Hay-on-Wye

If you are in need of somewhere to take children the **Small Breeds Farm Park and Owl Centre** a few miles south of Kington may provide an answer. The emphasis here is on allowing youngsters to get close to the animals – there are goats, rabbits, sheep, alpacas, horses and donkeys, guinea-pigs and miniature pigs, ducks, swans, geese, chipmunks, squirrels, tortoises and, if that wasn't enough, nearly thirty species of owl. The animals are friendly and many are used to being hand-fed by visitors and members of staff. The animals are housed in various fields and enclosures and if it is raining they can be viewed under cover. There is a cafe and an all-weather picnic area. Bring wellie-boots if it is wet underfoot.

Continuing southwards, if time and weather allow, it is worth a detour to the small village of **Almeley** – it is a peaceful place with a pub, The Bells, a church with some sixteenth century painted ceiling panels, and near the road junction to the north of the church is a scale plaque of the parish, cast for the millennium. In addition there are some old houses and great views over the surrounding countryside to the Black Mountains.

Further down the A4111 is the village of **Eardisley,** well known for its black and white timbered buildings, including the Tram Inn, which stands on the main road at the northern end of the village in what used to be the main market area and is named after the nineteenth century Brecon to Kington horse-drawn tramway. In addition the New Strand Cafe and Bookshop is something of a draw and there is also an old Pump House and some cruck cottages at this end of the village. However, at the southern end stands the Church of St. Mary Magdalene and this contains an extraordinary example of Herefordshire Romanesque Carving on its early twelfth century font. The main scene depicts the Harrowing of Hell – Christ, holding a cross with a dove on his shoulder, is pulling the hand of a small figure, identified as Adam, with the additional figures of a lion, representing evil, and God the Father holding a book. A second scene shows a pair of armed men fighting and is thought to be a possible reference to a duel fought between two local families, the Baskervilles and the Cliffords. If a walk is required, the Herefordshire Trail passes through the village and it is a pleasant walk along this route to the settlement of Lower and Upper Welson, before circling round on paths and lanes to Almeley and back to Eardisley.

The A438 follows the north bank of the River Wye through the village of **Whitney** before passing into Wales soon after the turn for Clifford along the B4350, which takes perhaps a more scenic route to the town of Hay. This road crosses the Wye on a wooden toll bridge. This is the fourth bridge to be

Top: Eardisland Village Above: 12th century font, Church of St. Mary Magdalene, Eardisley Above right: Hay-on-Wye Below: Castle Bookshop, Hay-on-Wye

built since a crossing was made in the eighteenth century. The first three had all been washed away by the end of that century, and the effort brought financial ruin to the builders, but the current stone and wooden construction has withstood the waters of the Wye ever since. A closer look of the bridge can be gained from the footpath running along the river's south bank. The village of **Clifford** has a castle – a motte and bailey dating from Norman times still with the remains of a twin-towered gatehouse. Unfortunately the site is on private ground and members of the public have to be satisfied with viewing it at a distance.

The town of **Hay-on-Wye** lies right on the English-Welsh border, and literally so as now the centre and the western parts of the town lie in Wales, while some houses in the eastern part are in England. In fact, the town used to be known as English Hay and the countryside to the west of the town as Welsh Hay, with the Welsh name for the town being Y-Gelli, which means 'grove'. For centuries it was a market town surrounded by its walls, of which only a trace remains along the town's northern edge above Newport Street (the B4350), and dominated by the Norman castle, whose walls and keep, albeit subsequently significantly altered, still tower over Castle Street. However, it is now best known for its plethora

Black Mountains, northern ridges

of bookshops. New, secondhand and antiquarian shops litter the town and you can find just about any volume you would wish in the thirty or so that now operate here – even the Castle and the Old Cinema have been converted. Perhaps the best way for bibliophiles to sample what is on offer is to start at one end of the town and work their way through them all. Situated at the top end of the town, on Oxford Road, are the main car park and the tourist information centre, where various leaflets about the town are available, including one which lists all the booksellers.

As if the bookshops were not enough, for ten days at the end of May and the start of June over the last twenty years or so something of an invasion has taken place by writers, performers, and general literary types coming to the town for the annual Hay Festival. The talks and events all used to take place right in the centre of the town, but the festival has outgrown the place and is now held in tented fields a little outside Hay. However, the festival has retained its essential remit and the concept has now been exported around the world – should you wish, you can attend sister-festivals in Spain, Africa, and even the Maldives. The town also has a most extraordinary official sibling, being twinned with the ancient literary centre of Timbuktu.

If books are not for you or as literary respite, the Black Mountains are not far away. The hill of Hay Bluff overlooks the town. You can walk all the way to the top following Offa's Dyke Path, or take the car most of the way on the steep road which leads to some parking areas below the hills's upper slopes, and beyond over the Gospel Pass and down to Capel-y-ffin and Llanthony Priory in the Vale of Ewyas in Monmouthshire.

Towards the Golden Valley

East of Hay and lying to the south of the A438 in the Wye Valley on the B4352 are the easily bypassed villages of **Bredwardine** and **Brobury**. However, there are a number of good reasons for detouring here. The churchyard at Bredwardine contains the grave of the vicar and diarist Francis Kilvert; there's an old motte and bailey castle; a beautiful bridge spans the Wye and there are some gardens open to the public, as well as a seventeenth century brick-built former coaching inn, The Red Lion, which now stands on the route of the Wye Valley Walk.

St. Andrew's Church, **Bredwardine**, lies between the village crossroads and the river at the end of a short lane. Francis Kilvert is the reason many stop to visit – he was vicar here for the last two years of his life and lived in the nearby vicarage. You'll find his grave on the north side of the churchyard. On the north wall you can see some interesting herring-bone masonry and the misaligned walls may indicate that the building originally comprised of separate structures. There is also a monument to Robert Vaughan, who died at Agincourt, defending Henry V. A short walk past the church brings you to the now overgrown site of the old castle, though the earthworks can still be made out.

The eighteenth century bridge across

the River Wye deserves notice in its own right, being one of the oldest brick-built examples still standing, and can be viewed by walking along the footpath on the west bank. Just beyond the bridge up the hill lies the entrance to **Brobury House Gardens**. The original gardens here date from the 1880s when the house was built and the air of a Victorian terraced garden is still very much apparent, though since 2001 the current owners, the Cartwrights, in conjunction with the designer Peter Antonius, have considerably restored and extended what there is to see and experience. There are five varied acres/2ha to explore, from formal areas near the house through stands of mature trees of chestnuts, pines, cedars and oaks, and down to watermeadows bordering the River Wye. There are also orchards, formal water features, seats for taking in the views across the river and a vegetable garden which was once worked by Francis Kilvert – there is even a mulberry tree planted by him which still thrives. Design is clearly an integral feature here and has been applied strikingly, though still in keeping with the imposing backdrop of the turreted Victorian house – and if additional interior inspiration is required, you can visit Jan Baker's Fabrics and Home shop in the Old Coach House.

If a walk in the area is needed, you can get some air into your lungs by climbing the Wye Valley Walk footpath that rises steeply westwards from the centre of Bredwardine to the top of Merbach Hill before bearing southeast to **Arthur's Stone** – a neolithic burial chamber thought to be over 4,000 years old – and back northwards to Bredwardine. On a clear day the views from the high ground extend over the Black Mountains and deep into Monmouthshire.

The valley to the south is known as the **Golden Valley**. The river here is the Dore, an unusual name, possibly from the French *or*, though the etymology is more likely to be from the Welsh, *dwr*, meaning water, or from *ystrad-our*, meaning place of gold. However, there may be a wholly natural and visual explanation for the name – try travelling through the valley on a late summer's evening when the fields are full of wheat about to be harvested.

Be that as it may, commanding the head of the valley is the splendid village of **Dorstone**. There is a triangular village green with a market cross, topped by a sundial; the school is now the village hall; and behind this is a motte and bailey castle to explore. The pub, the Pandy Inn, is still thriving, and has been since Sir Richard de Brito in the twelfth century built an inn here during his construction of the village church as part of his penance for the murder of Archbishop Thomas a Beckett in Canterbury Cathedral in 1170, making it perhaps the oldest pub in the county. The current church is the third on the site and dedicated to St. Faith – likely to have been identified with the Celtic Saint Moy, which to Norman ears was similar to *Foi*, and hence 'Faith'. The church also used to have a rare thirteenth century coffin chalice, though this was stolen in 2005 and only an old picture of it remains. Look out for more sundials on the approach to the church, this time in the form of stone balls on the churchyard

Bredwardine Bridge

Above: Arthur's Stone

gateposts. Also in the village is a new children's playground and an innovative community centre known as Dorstone's Front Room, with a shop, meeting area and exhibition space for artists.

A little way south of **Peterchurch**, which has an impressive aisleless Norman church, just off the B4347 lies the quiet village of **Vowchurch**. Set on the banks of the River Dore, there is a bridge with a convenient bench, a church and an old timber-framed house across the churchyard to draw the eye. The church of St. Bartholomew has a black and white bell tower and inside there are huge oak pillars supporting the equally impressive roof beams. On the Jacobean screen are two crudely carved figures, supposedly of Adam and Eve, and some dragons.

In fact, this area seems to attract unusual features in its churches. At **Michaelchurch Escley** there is a wall-painting of 'Christ of the Trades' – dressed in a loin cloth and surrounded by tradesmen's tools, this is thought to represent a warning to Sabbath breakers – while on the window sill to the right of the altar is a curious triangular slab of stone inscribed with sun, moon, stars, sheaves, and a book. **St. Margaret's** is famous for a pre-Reformation screen

Above: Dore Abbey

Above: Abbey Dore Court

Above right: Gospel Pass, Black Mountains

and eighteenth century wall texts, and **Bacton** for its dedication to St. Faith and its association with Blanche Parry, the Chief Gentlewoman of Queen Elizabeth I's Privy Chamber and Keeper of Her Majesty's Jewels – there is a monument to them both to the left of the altar. Also here are wall tablets, dedicated to two sons of the Partridge family, unusual for their coloured military ribbon decorations. A few miles to the south lies the Norman church of **Rowlestone,** whose chancel arch and south doorway provide some fine examples of the Herefordshire School of Romanesque Carving.

However, the main religious building in the Golden valley is **Dore Abbey**. Only the presbytery, crossing and transepts survive of the original, much more extensive, abbey but it still looks imposing, set as it is in a secluded position. It was founded by French monks of the Cistercian order in the twelfth century, and is notable for being the only abbey in England founded by the mother house of Morimond. Despite being dissolved in the sixteenth century much of interest survives inside, not least because of the restoration by John Scudamore in the 1600s. Scudamore was a close friend of Archbishop William Laud who closely influenced much of the remodelling; their coats of arms are placed on the Oak Screen either side of that of Charles I. There are plenty of arresting features and artefacts, including the intact stone altar, wall paintings, ceiling bosses, side chapels, inscriptions, a poor box dated 1639, medieval graffiti on some of the pillars and a grim painting of a skeleton with the motto 'memento mori'. More recently, the Friends of Dore Abbey, in association with English Heritage, have ensured that the buildings and its treasures are still cared for and open to public view.

Nearby lies **Abbey Dore Court** whose garden is open to the public. When the Ward family arrived here in the 1960s much of what is now garden was covered in brambles, trees and bindweed or indeed was fields. Since 1976 the gardens have evolved little by little and the result now is an informal and peaceful setting by the banks of the River Dore and framed by the house itself. There are a field garden, the long borders, a wild garden, and, across an ornate bridge over the river, the delightful Stephen's Meadow with some young and unusual trees, while adjacent to the house is a walled garden with nine individual borders. There is a small nursery specialising in herbaceous perennials and some newly restored tearooms in the house's former coaching yard. Combined with the setting, surrounded as it is by stunning landscape, there is a real sense of place here, and how could it not be - the Cistercians thought so long ago and built an abbey on the far side of the river and the Romans were here before them building roads and very possibly a number of villas along the valley.

The Upper Monnow Valley

The Gospel Pass road southwards from Hay-on-Wye soon reaches a left turn to Longtown and bears round the north side of Hay Bluff and Black Hill.

Just past the high point of the road, at 483yds/442m, a farm lane leads off steeply downhill to Abbey Farm and a stream which feeds the River Monnow further down the valley. Here, through a gate opposite some barns, lie the ruins of **Craswall Priory** on the southern slopes of Cefn Hill. Despite the wild surroundings, the priory must have flourished – there were cloisters, a church, chapter house, various other buildings, a fishpond and a spring. The priory was one of three houses in Britain founded in the thirteenth century by the French order of Grandmont but records suggest it was suppressed in the fifteenth century.

A mile further down the valley stands the current **parish church of Craswall, St. Mary's**. It is built low and solid, no doubt designed to withstand the rigours of the mountain weather. Inside the church is divided in an unusual way, with the vestry at the west end. This used to be a schoolroom and that may explain the area on the exterior of the north wall, which is thought to have been used as a fives court. There is also a curious hollow in the north-west corner of the churchyard, which may well have been a cock-fighting pit. Noticeable is the absence of gravestones here – the bedrock lies just beneath the surface and must make the churchyard unsuitable for burials.

The way down the valley through **Craswall** gives a wonderful run, especially on a bicycle, and the vista along the north scarp of the Black Mountains is something to be seen, and even more impressive in gloomy weather when the hills positively glower and earn their reputation. At **Longtown** are the ruins of its castle, built originally in the twelfth century and with its round keep reminiscent of the castle at Skenfrith. There is also an outer curtain wall and plenty of corners for children, young and and not so young, to explore, despite English Heritage's doom-mongering safety signs.

The last village before the border is **Clodock**. Its church has box pews, a three tier pulpit and an imposing decalogue wall painting on the north wall opposite the south doorway. To the rear the River Monnow runs over some small cascades.

A left turn over the bridge towards **Walterstone** soon leads up the side of the valley to the **Monnow Valley Arts Centre**. Founded in 2007 in a magnificent elevated position looking south across the River Monnow to the Black Mountains, the centre houses two galleries in a converted stone barn and 13ac/5ha of sculpture garden are being developed, showing works by artists of national and international repute. On display inside is a series of changing exhibitions of contemporary and modern landscape painting and photography. The centre also includes an artist's studio, where visiting artists can work and stay. It is a bold venture but one that is attracting serious collectors and patrons, eager to display their art collections against the backdrop of one of the most inspiring landscapes in Britain.

Places to Visit

Around Kington

Kington Museum
Mill Street, HR5 3AL
☎ 07974 526397 / 01544 231486
www.kingtonmuseum.co.uk
Local collections of photographs, domestic items, implements,and textiles
Open: Apr–Sep, Tue-Sat 10.30-4
Location: Kington centre

Hergest Croft Gardens
Kington, HR5 3EG
☎ 01544 230160
www.hergest.co.uk
gardens@hergest.co.uk
Family managed garden with 5,000 rare trees and shrubs extending over 70 acres with views to the Black Mountains
Tearoom, shop, plant sales
Open: weekends in Mar, daily Apr–Oct, 12-5.30
Location: ½ mile west of Kington along Ridgebourne Road

Westonbury Mill Water Gardens
Pembridge, HR6 9HZ
☎ 01544 388650
www.westonburymillwatergardens.com
richardpim@btinternet.com
Hydrologist designed water gardens extending over 3 acres with unusual features
Tearoom, plant sales
Open: Easter-Sep,11-5 (daily)
Location: 1½ miles east of Kington off A44

Small Breeds Farm Park and Owl Centre
Kington, HR5 3HF
☎ 01544 231109
www.owlcentre.com
Open: Summer 10.30-5.30 (daily); Winter 10.30-4 (daily)
Location: 2 miles south of Kington off A4111

Around Pembridge

Old Chapel Gallery
Pembridge, HR6 9HB
☎ 01544 388842
www.oldchapelgallery.co.uk
oldchapelgallery@googlemail.com
Open: 11-5 (daily)
Location: East Street, Pembridge

Eardisland Georgian Dovecote
Eardisland
Open all year, daily
Admission free

Dunkerton's Cider Mill
Pembridge HR6 9ED
☎ 01544 388653
www.dunkertons.co.uk
Family run cider mill and shop with chocolate patisserie
Open: Mon–Sat 10-5
Location: 1 mile south of Pembridge

The Golden Valley

Brobury House Gardens
Brobury, HR3 6BS
☎ 01981 500229
www.broburyhouse.co.uk
enquiries@broburyhouse.co.uk
Victorian terraced garden with modern landscaping on banks of River Wye
Open: all year, 10-5 (daily)
Location: ½ mile from Bredwardine off B4352 or A438 between Hay-on-Wye and Hereford

Dore Abbey
Abbey Dore, HR2 0AA
☎ 01981 570251 / 240618
www.doreabbey.org.uk
Former Cistercian monastery founded by French monks in the 12th century
Programme of concerts and music festival
Open: 9–dusk (daily)
Location: on B4347 3 miles west of A465, between Pontrilas and Hay-on-Wye

Abbey Dore Court Gardens
Abbey Dore, HR2 0AD
☎ 01981 240419
www.abbeydorecourt.co.uk
6 acre plant lovers' garden, 4 acre meadow with unusual trees
Teas served in courtyard
Open: weekends Apr–Sep 11-5 (most other times by request)
Location: just off B4347 3 miles west of A465, between Pontrilas and Hay-on-Wye

Monnow Valley Arts Centre
Walterstone, HR2 ODY
☎ 01873 860529
www.monnowvalleyarts.org
info@monnowvalleyarts.org
Gallery and 13 acre sculpture garden set against a backdrop of the Black Mountains
Open: Apr–Nov, Thu-Fri 11-6, Sat-Sun 2-5 (other times by arrangement)
Location: 3 miles north of Pandy off A465

Fact File

Getting Around

By Air

The nearest international airport is Birmingham, with Cardiff, Bristol, and Manchester also within reach.

By Car

Journey time to Hereford is 3 hrs from London and 1½ hrs from Birmingham; access via the motorways M4 or M5/M50.
Distances to Hereford: from Birmingham 58 miles, London 135 miles, Manchester 138 miles, Cardiff 56 miles.

Car Hire – Birmingham Airport

Avis Rent A Car ☎ 08445 810170
Budget Rent-a-Car ☎ 0844 581 2251
Europcar ☎ 0121 782 6507
Hertz Rent-a-Car ☎ 0121 661 3324
National Car Rental ☎ 0121 661 8757

Car Hire – Local firms

Alamo Rent A Car ☎ 01432 279202
Baynham Self Drive ☎ 01432 273298
Enterprise Rent A Car ☎ 0870 350 3000
Europcar ☎ 01432 801481
Hertz Rent-a-Car ☎ 01432 508660
United Rental System ☎ 01432 801145

By Rail

There are railway stations located at Hereford, Leominster, Ledbury and Colwall.
From Birmingham International Airport trains run regularly into Birmingham New Street Station and on to Hereford.
From Central London (Paddington Station) travel via Newport to Hereford and Leominster.
National Rail Enquiries ☎ 08457 484950, www.nationalrail.co.uk
Arriva Trains ☎ 08457 484950, www.arrivatrainswales.co.uk
Central Trains www.centraltrains.co.uk
Great Western Trains www.great-western-trains.co.uk
London Midland ☎ 0121 634 2040, www.londonmidland.com
The Man in Seat 61, www.seat 61 (a non-commercial enquiries site set up by rail expert Mark Smith)

By Coach

National Express Coaches (☎ 08717 818178, www.nationalexpress.com) operates from London and Birmingham to Hereford, Ledbury and Ross-on-Wye.

By Bus

Local bus enquiries: ☎ 01432 260211, www.herefordshire-buses.tbctimes.com
National bus enquiries: Traveline ☎ 0871 200 22 33

By Bike

Sustrans ☎ 0845 113 0065, www.sustrans.org.uk
Cycle Touring Club ☎ 0844 736 8450, www.ctc.org.uk
Cycle Hereford cyclehereford.com
Wheely Wonderful Cycling ☎ 01568 770755, www.wheelywonderfulcycling.co.uk

Maps

The Ordnance Survey produces excellent maps for car travel, walking and cycling:
OS Road Map 6 Wales and West Midlands 1:250 000
OS Landranger 148 Presteigne and Hay-on-Wye 1:50 000
OS Landranger 149 Hereford and Leominster 1:50 000
OS Landranger 150 Worcester and the Malverns 1:50 000
OS Landranger 161 Abergavenny and the Black Mountains 1:50 000
OS Landranger 162 Gloucester and the Forest of Dean 1:50 000
OS Explorer 189 Hereford and Ross-on-Wye 1:25 000
OS Explorer 190 Malvern Hills and Tewkesbury 1:25 000
OS Explorer 201 Knighton, Presteigne and Kington 1:25 000
OS Explorer 202 Leominster and Bromyard 1:25 000
OS Explorer 203 Ludlow and Tenbury Wells 1:25 000
OS Oudoor Leisure 13 Brecon Beacons – Eastern area 1:25 000
OS Outdoor Leisure 14 Wye Valley and Forest of Dean 1:25 000

Where to Get Information

Working in partnership with Herefordshire Council is the organisation ***Visit Herefordshire*** (☎ 01432 260621 or enquiries@visitherefordshire.co.uk). This organisation produces a large number of leaflets and guides for those visiting the county. Much of the information they disseminate is provided by individual businesses and establishments themselves. They also maintain a website at www.visitherefordshire.co.uk.
Local tourist information centres are an invaluable source of information and advice for visitors and the county is well served with centres in all the major towns and some of its villages.

Tourist Information Centres

Bromyard
The Bromyard Centre, Cruxwell Street
☎ 01432 260280

Hay-on-Wye
Oxford Road, ☎ 01497 820144

Hereford
1 King Street, ☎ 01432 268430

Kington
2 Mill Street, ☎ 01531 636147

Ledbury
The Masters House, St. Katherines
☎ 01531 636147

Leominster
1 Corn Square, ☎ 01568 616460

Queenswood Country Park
Dinmore Hill, ☎ 01568 797842

Ross-on-Wye
Edde Cross Street, ☎ 01989 562768

Libraries

The Bromyard Centre
1 Cruxwell Street, Bromyard, HR7 4EB
☎ 01432 260280

Hereford Library
Broad Street, Hereford, HR4 9AU
☎ 01432 383600

The Kington Centre
64 Bridge Street, Kington, HR5 3DJ
☎ 01432 260600

Ledbury Library
Bye Street, Ledbury, HR8 2AA
☎ 01531 632133

Leintwardine Library
Community Centre, High Street, Leintwardine, SY7 0LZ,
☎ 01547 540459

Leominster Library
8 Buttercross, Leominster, HR6 8BN, ☎ 01432 383290

Ross Library
Cantilupe Road, Ross-on-Wye, HR9 7AN
☎ 01432 383280

Sightseeing, Leisure and Entertainment

Tour Guides and Sightseeing

Bicycle Beano
☎ 01982 560471

Celtic Trails Walking Holidays
☎ 01291 689 774

Drover Holidays
☎ 01497 821134

Marches Tour Guides
☎ 01981 550150

Walk Herefordshire
☎ 01568 614411

Theatres

Bromyard

Conquest Theatre
☎ 01885 488575

Hereford

Courtyard Centre for the Arts
☎ 01432 340555

Ledbury

The Market Theatre
☎ 01531 633760

Ross-On-Wye

Phoenix Theatre
☎ 01989 564570

Leisure Centres

Bromyard

The Bromyard Centre
Cruxwell St, Bromyard, Herefordshire
HR7 4EB
☎ 0845 2410980

Hereford

Hereford Leisure Centre
Holmer Rd, Hereford, Herefordshire HR4 9UD
☎ 0845 2410978

Kington

Lady Hawkins Community Leisure Centre
Park Rd, Kington, Herefordshire HR5 3AG
☎ 01544 230488

Ledbury

Ledbury Leisure Centre
Mabels Furlong, Ledbury, Herefordshire
HR8 2HF
☎ 0845 2412579

Leominster

Bridge Street Sports Centre
Bridge St, Leominster, Herefordshire
HR6 8EA
☎ 0845 2410972

Leominster Leisure Centre
Coningsby Rd, Leominster, Herefordshire
HR6 8LL
☎ 0845 2412540

Golf Courses

Hereford

Belmont Lodge and Golf Course
Belmont HR2 9SA
☎ 01432 352666

Brockington Hall Golf Club
Bodenham, HR1 3HX
☎ 01568 797877

Burghill Valley Golf Club
Hereford, HR4 7RW
☎ 01432 760456

Hereford Municipal Golf Course
Hereford, HR4 9UD
☎ 01432 344376

The Herefordshire Golf Club
Hereford, HR4 8LY
☎ 01432 830219

Opposite page: Bromyard Folk Festival

Kington

Kington Golf Club
Kington HR5 3RE, ☎ 01544 230340

Leominster

Grove Golf and Bowl Centre
Leominster, HR6 0LE
☎ 01568 615333

Leominster Golf Club
Leominster, HR6 0LE
☎ 01568 612863

Ross-on-Wye

Ross-on-Wye Golf Club
Ross On Wye, HR9 7UT
☎ 01989 720267

South Herefordshire Golf Club
Ross On Wye, HR9 7UA
☎ 01989 780535

Hay-on-Wye

Summerhill Golf Course
Hay On Wye, HR3 5EW
☎ 01497 820451

Herefordshire Markets

Farmers Markets

Hereford Saturday Market: 1st Sat each month, 9-3, High Town
Hereford Thursday Market: 3rd Thu each month, 9-2, High Town
Leominster Market: 2nd Sat each month, 9-1, Corn Square
Ross Market: 1st Fri each month, 9-1, Market Hall

Retail Markets

Hereford Buttermarket, High Town, Mon-Sat every week
Hereford Retail Market, Cattle Market, Weds & Sat
Kington Open Market, Kington Hall, every Tue
Leominster Open Market, Corn Square, every Fri
Ledbury Country Market, St. Katherine's Hall, every Fri
Ross-on-Wye Open Market, Market Place, every Thu & Sat

Festivals

Listed below are the main annual festivals and events in the county. For details of all events in the county see the seasonal leaflets ***Herefordshire Festivals and Events*** which are produced by Visit Herefordshire (☎ 01432 260621 or enquiries@visitherefordshire.co.uk).

Borderlines Film Festival: Feb-Mar
☎ 01432 340555
www.borderlinesfilmfestival.co.uk

The Big Apple – Blossomtime Celebration: May
☎ 01531 670544
www.bigapple.org.uk

International Cider and Perry Competition: May
☎ 01432 354207
www.cidermuseum.co.uk

Hereford Photography Festival: May-Jun
☎ 01432 351964
www.photofest.org

Hay Festival: May-Jun
☎ 0870 990 1299
www.hayfestival.com

Herefordshire Summer Walking Festival: Jun
☎ 01568 797842
queenswoodtic@herefordshire.gov.uk

Leominster Festival: Jun
☎ 01568 611553

Kington Festival: Jun
☎ 01544 231209
www.kingtonfestival.co.uk

Kington Rough Ride Mountain Bike Event: Jun
☎ 01544 230059
www.roughride.co.uk

Ledbury Poetry Festival: July
☎ 0845 458 1743
www.poetry-festival.com

Three Choirs Festival: Aug
☎ 0845 652 1823
www.3choirs.org

Herefordshire Festival of Fungi: Aug-Dec
☎ 01531 631736
www.herefordshire-fungi.org.uk

Herefordshire Food Festival: Oct
☎ 01432 260 621
www.herefordshirefoodfestival.com

Herefordshire Winter Walking Festival: Dec
☎ 01568 797842
queenswoodtic@herefordshire.gov.uk

Where to Stay

Hotels, Guest Houses and Bed & Breakfast

The following is a list of places in or near town centres which may be of use for those needing to arrange accommodation at short notice or for an unexpected stop-over. Inclusion in the list is not by itself meant as a recommendation. For a more detailed list of places to stay see the booklet ***Herefordshire and the Wye Valley***, produced annually by Visit Herefordshire (☎ 01432 260621 or enquiries@visitherefordshire.co.uk), which includes an accommodation section and is stocked in the county's tourist information centres. In addition, there are now many commercial websites able to provide detailed information and take bookings in advance.

Hereford

Alberta Guest House
☎ 01432 270313

Castle House Hotel
☎ 01432 356321

Cedar Guest House
☎ 01432 267235

Charades Guest House
☎ 01432 269444

Green Dragon Hotel
☎ 01432 272506

Somerville House
☎ 01432 273991

Town House B&B
☎ 01432 351109

Travelodge Hereford
☎ 0871 984 6343

Kington

Arrowbank Lodge B&B
☎ 01544 231115

Burton Hotel
☎ 01544 230323

Church House B&B
☎ 01544 230534

De Lacy House B&B
☎ 01544 231448

Lion Hotel
☎ 01544 231744

Oxford Arms Hotel
☎ 01544 230322

Swan Inn Hotel
☎ 01544 230510

Ledbury

Feathers Hotel
☎ 01531 635266

Redlands B&B
☎ 01531 634803

Russet House B&B
☎ 01531 630060

Talbot Hotel
☎ 01531 632963

Leominster

Best Western Talbot Hotel
☎ 0845 3130115

Copper Hall B&B
☎ 01568 611622

Lavender House B&B
☎ 01568 617559

Rossendale House B&B
☎ 01568 612 464

Royal Oak Hotel
☎ 01568 612610

Ross-On-Wye

Brookfield House B&B
☎ 01989 562188

King's Head Hotel
☎ 01989 763174

Linden Guest House
☎ 01989 565373

Radcliffe Guest House
☎ 01989 563895

Royal Hotel
☎ 01989 565105

White House Guest House
☎ 01989 763572

Youth Hostels

Kington YHA
☎ 01629 592700

Leominster YHA
☎ 01629 592700

Welsh Bicknor YHA
Goodrich
☎ 01629 592700

Camping and Caravan Parks

The following list is a selection of places which are available. Inclusion in the list is not by itself meant as a recommendation.

Hereford and the South

Lucksall Caravan & Camping Park Mordiford
☎ 01432 870213

Broadmeadow Touring Caravan & Camping Park
Ross-On-Wye
☎ 01989 768076

Doward Park Camp Site
Symonds Yat West, Ross-On-Wye
☎ 01600 890438

Elmsdale Touring Caravan And Camping Site
Symonds Yat West, Ross On Wye
☎ 01600 890782

Haywood Farm Caravan And Camping Park
Gorsley, Ross On Wye
☎ 01989 720453

Ledbury, Bromyard and the East

The Rock Caravan Park
Winslow, Bromyard
☎ 01885 482630

Saltmarshe Castle Caravan Park
Bromyard
☎ 01885 483207

Eastnor Castle
Ledbury, Deer Park
☎ 01531 633160

Orchard Yurt Putley
☎ 07751 724379
Pixley End Caravan & Camp Site, Trumpet, Ledbury ☎ 07968 160168
Woodside Lodges Country Park, Ledbury
☎ 01531 670269

Leominster and the North

Riverside Caravan Site
Leominster
☎ 01568 612095

Home Farm, Bircher
Leominster
☎ 01568 780525

Townsend Touring & Camping Park,
Pembridge
☎ 01544 388527

Pearl Lake Leisure Park
Shobdon
Leominster
☎ 01568 708326

The Beeches Campsite
Shobdon
Leominster
☎ 01568 708678

Frome Valley Vineyard and grapes

Right: Vat House with the Master cider maker at Weston's Cider

Kington and the West

Fleece Meadow Caravan & Camping Park
Kington
☎ 01544 231235

Midway Holiday Park
Aymestrey
☎ 01568 709319

Hollybush Camping
Hay-on-Wye
☎ 01497 706008

Radnors End Camping
Hay-on-Wye
☎ 01497 820780

Poston Mill Holiday Park
Golden Valley, Peterchurch
☎ 01981 550225

Food and Drink

All the county towns and many of the villages have a good range of places to eat and drink. Where an attraction has a cafe or tearoom this is usually mentioned in the relevant description and in the *Places to Visit* sections.
For specific information on where to eat a ***Directory of Food & Drink*** has been produced by Herefordshire Food Links (☎ 01432 294114, www.herefordshirefoodlinks.org.uk) in association with the Bulmer Foundation and Herefordshire Council. The booklet has information on producers, retailers, markets, and an Eating Out section featuring eateries within the county which specialise in using locally produced ingredients in their meals.

The Flavours of Herefordshire Award Scheme has been developed to encourage Herefordshire restaurants, pubs, B&Bs, tearooms and shops to serve and promote local food and drink. Businesses are judged on the amount of produce they source within forty miles of their business and the way in which they use this local food to create imaginative menus reflecting the distinctive cuisine of Herefordshire. The organisation also runs the annual Herefordshire Food Festival in October. For details or a leaflet listing the awards and the festival events contact Visit Herefordshire (☎ 01432 260621 or enquiries@visitherefordshire.co.uk).

S

T

V

W

Y

Published in the UK by:
Horizon Editions Ltd
Trading as The Horizon Press,
The Oaks, Moor Farm Road West, Ashbourne, Derbyshire DE6 1HD
e-mail stella@thehorizonpress.co.uk

1st Edition

ISBN 978-1-84306-494-7

British Library Cataloguing in Publication Data:
A catalogue record for this book is available from the British Library

Printed by: Gomer Press Limited, Llandysul, Ceredigion, Wales
Cartography and Design: Mark Titterton

Picture Credits:

Front cover: Eastnor Castle (Nigel Harriman)
Back Cover top: Weobley Village
Back Cover bottom: Leominster Priory

Courtesy of Visit Herefordshire: www.visitherefordshire.co.uk tel: 01432 260621
p.6, p.10, p.11, p.26, p.35 top, p.38, p.87, p.91 top & middle

Reproduced by kind permission of the Dean and Chapter of Hereford: p.18 top

Chris Gilbert: p.22 and p.51 bottom

Lindsey Porter: p.7 bottom, p.23, p.46, p.50 top-right, p.51, p.58 left, p.70, p. 79 top & bottom-left

Nigel Harriman: Front Cover and p.39

Courtesy of Weston's Cider: p.34 top and p.91 bottom

Courtesy of Dunkerton's Cider Mill: p.70 left

All other photography by the author